# BRACKETT'S BATTALION

# BRACKETT'S

## Minnesota Cavalry in the
## Civil War and Dakota War

# BATTALION

*Kurt D. Bergemann*

**BOREALIS
BOOKS**

Borealis Books is an imprint of the Minnesota Historical Society Press.

www.borealisbooks.org

The Minnesota Historical Society Press is a member of the Association of American University Presses.

Manufactured in the United States of America

10  9  8  7  6  5  4  3  2  1

∞  The paper used in this publication meets the minimum requirements of the American National Standard for Information Sciences—Permanence for Printed Library materials, ANSI Z39.48-1984.

International Standard Book Number 0-87351-477-7 (paper)

Library of Congress Cataloging-in-Publication Data

Bergemann, Kurt D.
    Brackett's Battalion : Minnesota cavalry in the Civil War and Dakota War / Kurt D. Bergemann.
        p.   cm.
    Rev. ed. of: Brackett's Battalion, Minnesota Cavalry, 1861–1866. 1996.
    Includes bibliographical references and index.
    ISBN 0-87351-477-7 (alk. paper)
    1.  United States. Army. Brackett's Battalion (1861–1866)—History.
    2.  Minnesota—History—Civil War, 1861–1865—Regimental histories.
    3.  United States—History—Civil War, 1861–1865—Regimental histories.
    4.  United States—History—Civil War, 1861–1865—Cavalry operations.
    5.  Tennessee—History—Civil War, 1861–1865—Cavalry operations.
    6.  Kentucky—History—Civil War, 1861–1865—Cavalry operations.
    7.   Dakota Indians—Wars, 1862–1865.
    I.  Bergemann, Kurt D. Brackett's Battalion, Minnesota Cavalry, 1861–1866.
    II.  Title.
E515.6.B73B47 2004
973.7'476—dc22
2003017276

Dedicated to my
Great-great-grandfather
ORIN J. SWAN
(1839–1937)
Company K · Fifth Iowa Cavalry
Company C · Brackett's Battalion, Minnesota Cavalry

# Brackett's Battalion

# INTRODUCTION

DURING THE AMERICAN CIVIL WAR of 1861 to 1865, Brackett's Battalion was an obscure unit of volunteer cavalry from a newly born state of the Union that produced only eleven regiments of infantry, two regiments and two battalions of cavalry, three batteries of light artillery, a regiment of heavy artillery, and two companies of sharpshooters. Yet Brackett's Battalion was among only a few volunteer units in the Union army to hold lengthy service on two vastly different war fronts. The only previous written history of Brackett's Battalion was published in the form of a short narrative more than one hundred years ago. A more comprehensive history is now recorded here for the first time.

Relative to the huge quantity of state, regimental, and other Civil War unit histories published since the war, and particularly since the one hundredth anniversary of the war, very little has been published on Minnesota's Civil War history. Perhaps the lack of books on Minnesota's role in the war is due to the state's geographic location and the news media of the time. With the exception of California and Oregon on the Pacific Coast, Minnesota stood in the far northwest corner of the United States and is still perceived to be far removed from the war in the South. Compared to its neighbor state Wisconsin, which supplied more than fifty regiments of volunteer infantry alone during the war, Minnesota with a small population produced just eleven regiments of infantry. This seemingly small number then of course would not have attracted as much attention in the war as other states.

Other northern states such as New York and Ohio together produced more than four hundred volunteer regiments of infantry and cavalry and numerous batteries of artillery. With states such as these contributing such large numbers of soldiers compared to smaller or less populated states, it stands to reason that the names of these states would appear most often in published histories on the Civil War. Likewise, newspaper correspondents covering the war would focus their attention on regions where the battles were being fought and also most often would mention the names of regiments from those more populated states simply because of their majority presence.

After the war, most if not all states, North and South, published histories of their volunteer units for libraries and historical institutions. Iowa's Civil War unit narratives are published in several volumes, whereas Minnesota's unit narratives are contained in only one volume. *Minnesota in the Civil and Indian Wars, 1861–1865,* was authorized by the Minnesota legislature in 1890. The book was distributed to all of the Minnesota Civil War veterans who could be found. The remaining copies were intended to be made available for sale to the general public, but most of those copies instead ended up with various historical societies and other libraries. Many of them were housed in the basement of the Minnesota Historical Society where they suffered from neglect. Since that time an occasional short story on Minnesota's involvement in the war, often written by a veteran, would appear in periodicals. Only a very small number of comprehensive Minnesota Civil War unit histories have been published.

The unfortunate occurrence of armed conflict on any level cannot be overstated, and we must be cautious in our glorification of militarism. The Civil War was a sad and unfortunate time in American history. A large part of the American population perished in the war. As in all wars, young men died in the prime of their lives, and families were torn apart all for what both sides in the conflict believed was a just cause. But the outcome of that war shaped the nation into what it is today. By reflecting on that bloody conflict, we can learn about where we are as a people and have been as a nation in the past and how we can continue to grow and mature. Minnesota's own history would not be complete without a proper account of its involvement in the Civil War.

For the last several years many Minnesota Civil War historians have been dismayed by the lack of updated, published histories on the subject. Much research has been done recently to improve the body of knowledge of Minnesota's role in the war, but little has been published in a complete and comprehensive manner. Many Minnesota regiments of the Civil War have extensive and proud histories, and there is a need, now more than ever, for those histories to be brought to the public forefront. A number of Minnesota historians have believed that the history of one volunteer unit in particular, Brackett's Battalion, is one of the best stories to illustrate Minnesota's role in the Civil War and that its history is "long overdue to be published" in an updated volume. The history of Brackett's Battalion is not a history of only the battalion itself, but because its service is so intertwined with other Minnesota units and Minnesota's mid-nineteenth century history, its story provides a broader account of Minnesota's presence in the war.

For the student of the Civil War who is interested in how the war itself was conducted, the history of Brackett's Battalion also provides a picture of the less-focused aspects of the conflict. Many of the broader histories of the war bring our attention to the famous battles, the devastation of those battles, and their overall results. But the activities of those obscure military units, operating behind the scenes, help us understand what was taking place across the countryside among the people of the South. The war was not just a few bloody patches of ground where major battles took place.

The story of Brackett's Battalion not only helps to enlighten us about Minnesota's role in the "war between the states," but more importantly emphasizes a dual role. The state's second role in the beginnings of what became known as the "Indian Wars" is often lost in Civil War history. Few books on the war allude to Minnesota's internal conflict with the native Dakota or Sioux. In August 1862, during the second year of the Civil War, Dakota warriors in Minnesota lashed out violently against Minnesota settlers and government Indian agents, thus thrusting the state into an internal war.

The bloody Dakota Conflict of 1862, also known as the Dakota War or in an earlier generation as the Sioux Uprising, was an inevitable outcome of the United States government and white settlers' determination to tame the West. After an estimated five hundred white men, women, and children as well as a number of mixed-blood and friendly Dakota were murdered and another one hundred Minnesota soldiers killed in the war, the conflict was brought to a halt after the Battle of Wood Lake in September. But that battle was not the end of hostilities between the government and the Dakota; it was just the beginning.

The era of the Indian Wars is often believed to be disconnected from the Civil War and separated in time as a post–Civil War period. On the contrary, the hostilities that existed between Indians and the U.S. government in the Northwest for more than thirty years was like a burning fuse long before 1862. The relationship between the Indians and Minnesota settlers had for years been an uneasy and sometimes volatile one. However, the settlers were fairly satisfied that the Indians were contained on reservations, which had been provided for them after much of Minnesota had been purchased from them.

It was the existence of Dakota and Lakota tribal groups to the west in Dakota Territory that made Minnesota settlers the most apprehensive about their safety. It was those tribes who for decades were known to be the most hostile toward white settlers and explorers. The fear and hostility regarding those Indians in the West was evident in the fall of 1861 when a committee of women from the settlements of Vernon, Winnebago, and Shelbyville in southern Minnesota presented the flag of the United States to the officers of one of the newly formed companies of Minnesota Cavalry. During the presentation, one of the women in her address to the men declared, "If you are ordered to one of our forts to protect our frontier and our homes from the blood-thirsty savages, *this* shall be your talisman to urge you on to victory."

Yet it was the Minnesota Dakota, starving from a crop failure and the reluctance of Indian agents to release food stores to them and the delay of funds owed to them from the purchase of their land, who ignited the war within the state in 1862. The next year, military campaigns against the Dakota were carried into the neighboring Dakota Territory. After two years in the South, Brackett's Battalion entered yet another campaign against the Dakota in 1864 as part of the Northwestern Indian Expedition, serving with other cavalry regiments from Minnesota and Iowa and two companies from Dakota Territory. In 1865 Brackett's Battalion returned to Dakota Territory for another expedition and remained there until the spring of 1866. The campaigns were intended to destroy the Indians' resistance to submission and make the western territories safe for settlement. But these measures, more often than not, only intensified hostilities.

The origins of the turbulence between the Indians and the U.S. government in the Northwest has been largely ignored in Civil War history due to the lack of attention it received at the time. President Abraham Lincoln and the federal government devoted as much time as they could to address the situation. But the war in the South, understandably, monopolized most of their attention, leaving many of the policy decisions to the military in dealing with the Indians. Likewise, national news coverage also focussed its attention on the more ominous conflict in the South. It is from those sources that many historians pulled much of the history of the Civil War, leaving the history of the other war in the Northwest as a mere footnote, if anything.

The story of Brackett's Battalion not only provides us with the many facts of regional and national conflicts, but it also illustrates a more confined history of soldiering for those students interested in the study of the soldier and tactics: Civil War cavalry history. The history of the Union cavalry during the Civil War was one of evolution, rather than one of an established branch of the military that was trained and poised for war duty at the outset. True, the United States had always utilized mounted troops as a part of its military. But due to improvements in the range and accuracy of the infantry rifle, Union commanders in the War Department at Washington, D.C., believed that the cavalry had become an obsolete branch of the military and was no longer a useful weapon in combat.

Shortly after the war had begun in April 1861 and after persuasive arguments from other Union leaders, the War Department reluctantly authorized the recruitment of volunteers for cavalry duty. It was not until the fall of that year that the first volunteer cavalry regiments were ready for the field. However, the northern volunteer cavalrymen were ill prepared for the kind of duty that would be required of them. The key elements of a cavalry are its weapons and its horses.

Northerners were not known for their horsemanship. It was impractical for most people of average means who resided in the towns and industrialized cities to keep and maintain a horse. On the farms, oxen and mules were most commonly employed to pull plows, wagons, and other implements. For those few who owned horses, the horse, if not a mule, was used to pull carriages, surreys, buckboards, or commercial vehicles.

Thus, the new Union volunteer cavalrymen were in for a rude awakening. They believed that life in the cavalry would be an easier, more glamorous duty than that of the infantry. After a few weeks in service they learned that it was anything but glamorous. Not only were few of them capable horsemen, but they also soon learned that the horses they were expected to manage with great skill were usually barely broken or not broken at all.

As for weapons, in ideal circumstances a typical cavalryman would be issued a saber, a revolver, and a breech-loading carbine. Armed as such, a cavalryman could provide a significant amount of fire power if he were trained properly. But during their first several months of service, many of these northern volunteer cavalry units suffered from the lack of an adequate supply of weapons and often entered the field of battle armed with only one weapon and that one frequently of poor quality.

Thrust into the field, poorly mounted on green horses of often questionable health, poorly armed, and with little training, the inexperienced cavalrymen took their mounts for granted. Many of them believed that the horse was an always reliable means of transportation that would do anything and take the rider anyplace under any circumstance. As a result, the volunteers' horses were poorly cared for. Few horses were lost from wounds on the battlefield compared with those lost due to the ignorance of officers and enlisted men as to the proper methods of caring for the animals. This prevented the Union cavalry, particularly in the western theater of the Civil War, from engaging in large-scale fighting for the first several months.

The Confederate cavalry, however, quickly gained a reputation as a formidable threat. They proved that their horsemanship skills and ability to engage in combat was superior to that of the northern horsemen. In the South, the lack of good roads had forced southerners to utilize horseback transportation from a young age. Equestrian sports were also a pastime for many southern men of all ages. When pressed into service, the volunteers were compelled to bring their own mounts as the Confederacy had little means to supply its cavalry with horses. This practice also provided a motivation for the men to keep their mounts in good condition.

As the Confederate cavalry rewrote the established methods of mounted tactics by making many daring raids behind federal lines, the Union cavalry slowly gained experience in the field. During the first several months of duty, the Union volunteer cavalry was engaged mostly in picket and patrol duties and on occasion would be involved in small-scale combat. Over time the northern cavalry played a more active role in major engagements, becoming a viable force against a weakening Confederate army. As the Union army pushed its way south in the last years of the war, devastating the southern economy and its ability to support its military, the northern horsemen finally achieved their day in the sun.

The history of Brackett's Battalion of Minnesota Cavalry is an accurate reflection of the evolution of volunteer cavalry during the Civil War. As the first Minnesota volunteer cavalry troops mustered for the war, these men were originally designated as the First, Second, and Third Companies of Minnesota Cavalry in the fall of 1861. The three companies were then mustered into a regiment of volunteer cavalry. Consisting of companies from other midwestern states, the regiment was named the Curtis Horse while in training at St. Louis, Missouri. Soon after, due to the large number of men who hailed from the state of Iowa, the regiment was renamed the Fifth Iowa Cavalry, much to the dissatisfaction of some of the Minnesota troops.

The Fifth Iowa served over a large part of western and central Tennessee, performing duties also in Kentucky, Mississippi, and Alabama. During their first year in the field, long, monotonous patrols over the countryside on a daily basis provided the experience that the regiment needed. By 1863 the Fifth Iowa had become a skilled fighting unit. Well armed and well mounted, it was ready for combat on a larger scale.

After two years in the South, the Fifth Iowa was veteranized and granted thirty days furlough. While at home in Minnesota in February 1864, the three Minnesota companies were removed from the Fifth Iowa to become an independent unit of Minnesota cavalry called Brackett's Battalion, named for its commander, Major Alfred B. Brackett who originally recruited the Third Company.

Beginning in the spring of 1864, Brackett's Battalion, with the addition of a fourth company, served for two more years as part of the Northwestern Indian Expedition in the unforgiving environment of the open prairie of Dakota Territory. As a response to the 1862 Dakota Conflict in Minnesota, which occurred while the men of Brackett's Battalion were serving with the Fifth Iowa Cavalry in the South, the expedition's battles with the Dakota were among the initial stages of a war that would continue for another two decades, known to history as the Indian Wars.

Much of the history of Brackett's Battalion is recorded in the diaries of Eugene Marshall. Marshall began his service as a private with the Third Company of Minnesota Cavalry in the fall of 1861, eventually rising to the rank of sergeant major of Brackett's Battalion. A keen observer of his surroundings and an avid writer, Marshall chronicled in his diary nearly everything he experienced on a daily basis. His observations provide a detailed record of the life of a soldier during the

Civil War and the effects the war had on the people of the South and their homes. While on the northern plains, Marshall recorded a vivid account of his march across a drought-stricken Dakota Territory and his contact with hostile Indians who fought to protect their lands. He was also fascinated with the cultures of tribes he encountered along the way who were friendly to whites.

Today, the diaries of Eugene Marshall are preserved in the archives of Duke University, Durham, North Carolina. In 1963, Clark G. Reynolds, a graduate student at Duke University, based his master's thesis on the Marshall war diaries. Reynolds's thesis contains a transcription of nearly all the diary entries. Most of Marshall's diary entries quoted in this history of Brackett's Battalion are from the Reynolds thesis. A few of the quotes from Marshall's entries of the last few months of 1864 and some of 1865 are from the actual diaries. Eugene Marshall was skillful with a pen and paper. For his writings used in the following pages, his spelling and punctuation errors, although few, have been corrected to focus attention on the content of his writing rather than the quality.

But Eugene Marshall was not the only member of Brackett's Battalion to record its history. Several of the men who served in the battalion penned their observations and experiences in diaries and letters to relatives and hometown newspapers during the war and after the war published their experiences in newspapers and various other periodicals. Their accounts as well as Marshall's have greatly contributed to the history in this volume. Thankfully their written accounts provide for us a better understanding of the un-glorified and less-than-honorable aspects of war and the life of a soldier during that time. Without firsthand written accounts such as these, we might still view the histories of such military units as glamorous. Many of these men, to some degree, understood that they were taking part in a event that would shape the course of American history and would be written about for generations after.

The men who served in the battalion and had volunteered in the fall of 1861 also provide a sample of the variety of personalities and attitudes among the Union soldiers. These men who came from varied backgrounds, many of whom were European immigrants, volunteered for the Union army out of youthful ignorance or were motivated by patriotic exuberance. Some of them were abolitionists who viewed the war as a means to end slavery while others held no sympathies for "Negroes." And yet some men saw their military service as a means to become a war hero and return home with a degree of fame and improved status in their community, while others simply joined up for a better income than what they were making on the farm. For those men who joined the battalion in 1864, many of them viewed their service as an opportunity to wage revenge on the Dakota who had murdered their friends or family in the conflict of 1862. But for those men who enlisted in the Minnesota cavalry in the fall of 1861, whatever their personal reasons, their underlying motive to fight against the Confederate rebellion was to help preserve the union of the United States.

# PART ONE

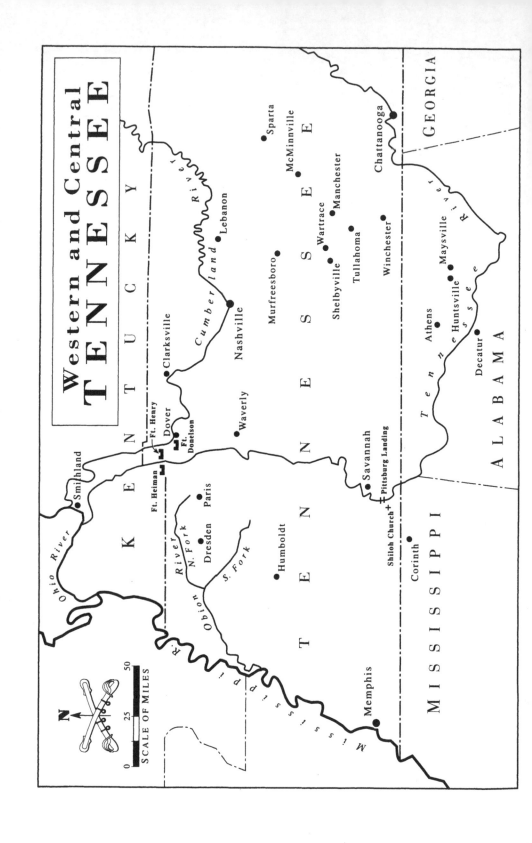

## Western and Central TENNESSEE

KENTUCKY

GEORGIA

Smithland

Ohio River

Ft. Heiman

Ft. Henry

Dover

Ft. Donelson

Clarksville

Cumberland River

Nashville

Waverly

Lebanon

Sparta

McMinnville

Manchester

Wartrace

Chattanooga

Murfreesboro

Shelbyville

Tullahoma

Winchester

Maysville

TENNESSEE

Paris

Dresden

N. Fork

Obion River

S. Fork

Humboldt

Savannah

Pittsburg Landing

Shiloh Church

Tennessee River

Athens

Huntsville

Decatur

ALABAMA

Corinth

MISSISSIPPI

Memphis

Mississippi R.

N

SCALE OF MILES

0    25    50

# The First Companies of Minnesota Cavalry in the Civil War

MINNEAPOLIS, MINNESOTA, was the host city of the annual National Encampment of the Grand Army of the Republic (GAR) in August 1906. Their numbers declining, the elderly Union veterans of the Civil War came from all over the country, gathering once again to rekindle their comradeship, swap stories of the war, and participate in the various festivities. In conjunction with the GAR event, the survivors of Brackett's Battalion held their own annual reunion at the old state capitol building in nearby St. Paul. Of the 150 surviving veterans of the battalion that year, seventy-two attended the reunion. This represented the largest attendance, as a percentage, of all the Minnesota units at the National Encampment.

During the battalion's reunion on August 14, the names of comrades who had passed away since the previous year's reunion were announced. Letters of greetings and well wishes from those unable to attend were read, including a letter from General Alfred C. Hawley, originally a corporal in the third company. The oldest survivor of the battalion that year, John Barnard at the age of eighty-eight, made the trip from Mankato. Still relying on crutches, Barnard was an ever-present reminder of the wounds and injuries that some of the men received in the war.

The once young and limber cavalry troopers, now old and gray, shook hands and embraced one another. Some had not seen each other in more than forty years. Seventeen of the men gathered the energy to march in the GAR's Grand Parade in Minneapolis the next day. William Seeger, the secretary of the Association of Survivors of the Minnesota Battalion, Fifth Iowa Cavalry and Brackett's Battalion, Minnesota Cavalry, wrote in his report about the parade, "though it was a very tedious wait before the start, and very hot, they marched once more, perhaps many of them for the last time, from start to finish; a little tired, but proud, satisfied and glad to have been together and had a bully good time."[1]

Anton Simonette, also at the reunion, remembered a longer march. His march had begun forty-five years earlier. He was the first Minnesota volunteer to be mustered in for cavalry duty during the first year of the Civil War. Anton was born in Switzerland and was a resident of St. Paul, Minnesota, when he was mustered into service as a volunteer on September 8, 1861 at the age of nineteen. Eight days later he was joined by sixteen more cavalry volunteers at Fort Snelling. Most of the new arrivals were German-born residents of St. Paul. This set the pattern for the First Company of Minnesota Volunteer Cavalry. Henning von Minden, a surveyor from St. Paul and a German immigrant, was recruiting other Germans from throughout the state. Many of von Minden's recruits were from Ramsey County, but he brought in men from wherever he could find them. Men from as far as Winona, Olmsted, and Sibley Counties answered the call to join the cavalry. Other men from the counties of Washington, Hennepin, Dakota, and Carver arrived at Fort Snelling to volunteer, seeking to bask in the glory of life as a dashing cavalryman.

By mid-October, ninety-eight volunteers had gathered at Fort Snelling to form the First Company. More than half of them were German immigrants. Many of them understood barely a word of English.

Von Minden, thirty-four years old, was mustered on September 29 and on October 14 was made captain of what became known as the "German company." Most of von Minden's officers, sergeants, and corporals were German born, including First Lieutenant August Matthaus, Second Lieutenant Gustave Leue, First Sergeant John G. Janicke, Sergeants Joseph Buck and William Robeck, along with five of the eight corporals.

Henning von Minden was known as a 48er in his former homeland. During the Danish-German civil war of 1848–51, von Minden served with the German army in a fight for independence from the Danish monarchy. After the revolution failed, von Minden followed exiled Germans to the United State in 1855 to start a new life. Now in 1861 von Minden committed himself to a new cause in his new home.

As the First Company began military instruction at the fort, they pondered the events that led them there. Few of them had expected to be at that place just a few months earlier. In April, Confederate artillery bombarded Fort Sumter in Charleston Harbor, South Carolina, then occupied by a small Federal garrison, igniting the "war between the states." The fort was surrendered and evacuated by the Federals as the northern states were left embittered and in shock.

However, people in the North were confident. Few believed the war would last much longer than three months. Minnesota Governor Alexander Ramsey happened to be in Washington during the siege on Fort Sumter and immediately offered one thousand troops from Minnesota to the Federal army, making Minnesota the first state to offer volunteers to the Union cause. Minnesota had been a state for only three years, and its population was low. The call for volunteers galvanized the patriotic enthusiasm of the citizens. The First Regiment of Minnesota Volunteer Infantry was quickly raised and mustered for three months of service and shortly after remustered for three years. As the First Regiment embarked for Washington, a second regiment was being raised.

On July 21 the First Minnesota Volunteers found themselves in the middle of the first major ground battle between Confederate forces and Federal troops near Manassas Junction and Bull Run Creek in Virginia. The battle, only twenty-five miles from Washington, D.C., was expected to be a quick and decisive victory for Federal troops, ending the war. But again the North was stunned as the Confederates routed the Union forces. The First Minnesota suffered the most casualties of all the Union regiments in the fight. People in the North began to realize this war would not be quick or bloodless.

The War Department then authorized Minnesota to raise more troops including three companies of cavalry. As Captain von Minden's first company was settling in at the once abandoned and now reoccupied Fort Snelling, the Second Minnesota Infantry Regiment steamed down the Mississippi River for duty in the South while a third regiment of infantry was being formed.

D. Mortimer West in Jackson County on Minnesota's southern border was gathering more cavalry volunteers. His efforts were restricted largely to close friends and relatives from the Norwegian-settled county. On October 22 and 23, West and his small group were mustered in at Fort Snelling.

Among them were the Olesons: Toloff, Peter, Simon, Ole E., and two Andrews all mustered on the twenty-second. On the twenty-third were the Wests: D. Mortimer, Stiles, Mate, James, and one known only as H. F. Nine days later, on November 1, the largest contingent of cavalry volunteers were mustered at the fort. Fifty-five men in all, mostly from Blue Earth and Faribault Counties in southern Minnesota, along with West's small group, began to form a second company of cavalry.

Many of the men from Blue Earth County were members of a county militia company called the Blue Earth County Cavalry, previously organized in May 1861. At that time it was believed that the Dakota Indians, the Sioux, might take advantage of the absence of so many men who had gone off to the war; therefore, the militia was formed. Most of the settlers of southern Minnesota held a great mistrust toward the Indians who lived in the area. Their fear of the Indians had been strengthened by the raids and murders a few Indians had committed four years earlier.

In 1857, a small band of lawless Dakota led by a man named Inkpaduta had brutally murdered more than thirty people at a small settlement in Dickinson County, Iowa, just across the southern Minnesota border. Crossing into Jackson County, Minnesota, the outlaw band then murdered several more people in the settlement of Springfield, later named Jackson. D. Mortimer West formed a company of Jackson County militia cavalry to pursue Inkpaduta. But the band and its leader were too elusive to capture. Shortly after, West's militia was disbanded.

But the people of Blue Earth County were still fearful after four years. However, when the call for volunteer cavalry to join the Union cause was made, many of the Blue Earth County cavalrymen felt it was a higher calling. Thirty-two men from Blue Earth County followed their captain, Benjamin F. Smith of Vernon, to Fort Snelling. There Smith was unanimously elected captain of the Second Company with West as first lieutenant. But before they were mustered, Smith was appointed lieutenant colonel of the Third Minnesota Infantry.

With the addition of a few more arrivals at the fort, the Second Company of Minnesota Cavalry consisted of eighty-six volunteers in all with the forty-four-year-old D. Mortimer West as their new captain. A former quartermaster sergeant from the First Minnesota regiment, William Smith, who had fifteen years of prior service in the U.S. Army, was appointed first lieutenant. Nathan Bass from Garden City, formerly a lieutenant of the Blue Earth County Cavalry, was appointed second lieutenant.

As von Minden and West were gathering their troops, Deputy

United States Marshal Alfred B. Brackett and Erwin Y. Shelley, a printer, teamed up to recruit a company of cavalry volunteers of their own. The two men from St. Paul placed ads in the local *Pioneer and Democrat* newspaper beginning in September calling for volunteers to join the "light cavalry" and to contact Shelley at his home for enlistment. Brackett, thirty-five years old, had built a reputation as a respected law man and skilled manhunter in Minnesota. Shelley, thirty-four years old, had some prior military experience. As a young man, Shelley had served with the Third U.S. Dragoons during the Mexican War of 1846–48.

Brackett and Shelley noted that von Minden was recruiting mostly German-born volunteers, and West's company came primarily from Blue Earth, Faribault, and Jackson Counties, many of whom were European immigrants or were born in New York like West. So Brackett and Shelley set out to give their company a distinction as well by recruiting volunteers born only in the United States.

Most of their recruits came from Hennepin and Ramsey Counties as well as from the neighboring counties to the south and southwest. But Brackett and Shelley were having difficulties gathering enough men for a full company, and time was running out. Minnesota was largely populated by European immigrants, and the number of enthusiastic American-born volunteers was running low.

On October 27, the military authorities in Minnesota received word from the War Department that a third company of cavalry from the state would not be required. Brackett and Shelley were greatly discouraged but were determined that their efforts would not be in vain. The men they had gathered were notified, and preparations were made the next morning to travel to Wisconsin. The First Wisconsin Cavalry Regiment under Colonel Edward Daniels was being mustered at Kenosha. Brackett, Shelley, and their volunteers decided they would join up with them and make the best of it. However, before they departed, they were notified of their salvation. Minnesota's adjutant general stepped in and agreed to muster in the small company at Fort Snelling. Their fate, however, was still undetermined.

On November 1 the men were mustered into service, the same day as most of West's company. Brackett and Shelley were mustered in on the fourth. Brackett was appointed captain and Shelley was first lieutenant. The remaining officers were yet to be determined. At this time,

Brackett still did not have enough troops for a full company. On November 5, a new ad appeared in the *Pioneer and Democrat*:

> Capt. Brackett's Cavalry wants a few more men to fill up to the minimum. All those who wish to enter this most attractive arm of the service can find no better company to join than this. It is composed of respectable young men of American birth who intend to make it the crack company of the State. Recruits will please report to Lieut. Shelley at the Fort.[2]

The ad helped. Brackett and Shelley spent the first part of the month securing more commitments. Finally enough additional recruits were brought in to fill the company. The Third Company of Minnesota Cavalry had ninety-two volunteers in all, of which only nineteen were foreign born.

Mortimer Neely, a twenty-seven-year-old clerk from St. Paul, was mustered on November 21. Neely saw this as an opportunity to make something of himself. He campaigned vigorously to secure a commission in the company despite the disgruntlement of some of the men who were more qualified but modest. Neely was successful nonetheless and was elected a second lieutenant. The formation of the three companies of Minnesota Cavalry was now complete.

For most of the men, military training at Fort Snelling was awkward and tiresome. They were citizen soldiers of whom many would not normally have sought a career in the military. The muster rolls for the three companies record merchants, printers, clerks, stage drivers, teachers, carpenters, lumbermen, teamsters, saddlers, blacksmiths, and many farmers. In Brackett's Third Company there was a sixteen-year-old former Pony Express rider by the name of Florence Garen. An Irish immigrant who had been living on his own for several years, Garen easily sold himself as an eighteen year old.

Sergeant William B. McGeorge of the Third Company was a lawyer from St. Paul who rose to the rank of second lieutenant during his four and one-half years with the company. In the Second Company, Isaac Botsford, from the town of Blue Earth in Faribault County, had just a few months earlier founded the first newspaper in the county called the *Blue Earth City News*. In its first issue, Botsford professed to being a Republican but vowed his paper would not take sides with any

political party. He did, however, promise that the paper would advo-
cate the abolition of slavery. Botsford sold his half of the paper to a new
partner, and then he joined the cavalry to have a more direct partici-
pation in freeing the slaves.

There was the twenty-nine-year-old farmer from Caledonia, Minnesota, by the name of Eugene Marshall. He had settled in the south-
eastern corner of Minnesota Territory in 1853 where he surveyed and
helped to organize the settlement of Caledonia in the center of Hous-
ton County. An intelligent young man who was consumed with reading and writing, Marshall was highly observant of his surroundings
and always kept a diary in which he recorded his thoughts and observations daily. His most important diary began when he cast his for-
tunes with Captain Brackett. Had Marshall joined the army in any
other state during the war, he most certainly would have received a
commission as an officer. But in Minnesota, if one did not have friends
in high political office, commissions were difficult to obtain, even when
the qualifications were superior to those who received commissions.

Originally, Marshall was offered a well-deserved commission with
the Fourth Minnesota Infantry Regiment, but the opportunity was
blocked by Lieutenant Governor Ignatius Donnelly who appointed
one of his political friends to the position. Marshall never got another
opportunity, so he joined Brackett's company as a private, seeking a
chance for adventure as a cavalryman.

In his diaries, Marshall recorded his respect for Brackett and his
demonstrated abilities as a commanding officer. But Marshall was often frustrated over the lack of competence in other officers and their
ability to lead troops no better than many privates. He slowly rose
through the noncommissioned ranks and eventually became sergeant
major and his commander's most trusted soldier.

Like Marshall, many of the men envisioned the cavalry as an opportunity for glory and adventure. The reputation of a saber-wielding
cavalryman on the back of a horse charging into the enemy was very
appealing. Also, thoughts of traveling on horseback from place to place
instead of marching long distances on foot, toting a knapsack and a
heavy musket like the infantry, were much more desirable.

In the three companies, the two oldest men were members of
the First Company and were forty-five years old—Corporal Herman

Wedekemper and Casper Cantini, the company wagoner. Sixteen men were over forty years of age. Altogether, the average age of the Minnesota cavalrymen was about twenty-six.

Life at Fort Snelling was a mixture of constant activity, boredom, and a struggle for health and comfort. A typical day was three meals, more or less edible, three roll calls, dress parade, and hours of military drill. Drill was a learning experience for officers and enlisted men alike. The officers knew no more about it than the rest of the men and in that way were a constant source of amusement and frustration for the rest. When it rained too hard or the snow fell too heavily, drill was canceled, leaving the men in the barracks with nothing to do.

Most of the men were not accustomed to living with so many other men in a confined space. In the enlisted barracks, thirty men lived in each of the small rooms with less than half as many bunks. The cramped quarters led to the spread of disease and lice. Solitude was difficult to find. With each day growing colder and winter approaching, warmth was also a rarity in spite of the crowded conditions. Most of the blankets were not adequate, and often there was not enough firewood for heat.

After several days or even weeks of waiting, uniforms and some equipment were finally issued. Each man received one overcoat, one cavalry jacket, one pair of pants, two pairs of wool socks, one pair of drawers, one pair of boots, one forage cap, one regulation Hardee hat with all the trimmings, one pair of shoulder scales, one haversack, one infantry knapsack, and one canteen. Now, at last, the volunteers began to take on the appearance of real soldiers.

Throughout the fall of 1861, local politicians and home town officials invited the various infantry and cavalry units in training at the fort to attend public demonstrations of support and receive well wishes. During the third week of November, Captain West and Lieutenant Bass traveled to Mankato to make speeches and receive a flag for the Second Company. The flag was a gift from the ladies of Shelbyville, Vernon, and Winnebago. During the presentation, Miss Libbie H. Miller of Shelbyville addressed the two men with a stirring and emotional speech remarking, "should you be called southward, to battle with the rebels, we ask you to protect it, and not to allow it to be dishonored by a touch from a traitor's hand as long as one of you can raise an arm or strike a sabre."[3] As the two officers received the flag, Governor Ramsey was at the fort reviewing the Second Company.

In December, West's and Brackett's companies spent nearly an entire day marching through the streets of St. Paul, receiving cheers and well wishes from the citizens. In the evening, the two companies dined at the city's International Hotel. There they were joined by a few state politicians who made patriotic speeches of encouragement and support to the men. The Minnesota cavalry troops were becoming famous, locally, even before they had received any real cavalry training.

# Cavalry Training at St. Louis and Joining a Regiment

THE SECOND AND THIRD COMPANIES barely knew Captain von Minden's First Company. On the day that most of West's and Brackett's volunteers were being mustered in at Fort Snelling, November 1, the German company boarded steamers at the levee below the fort and embarked down the Mississippi River for St. Louis, Missouri, where they would receive formal cavalry training.

Originally, von Minden's company was under orders to join three other German companies of cavalry from Iowa under the command of Captain Carl Schaffer de Boernstein. A large number of German immigrants had settled in Iowa. Most of them were former freedom fighters, like von Minden, veterans of the 1848 Danish-German conflict who followed their exiled leaders to America. Captain Boernstein was under assignment from General John C. Frémont, commander of Federal troops in Missouri, to form a battalion of German cavalry that would join the general's bodyguard, a regiment named the "Frémont Hussars." Frémont fancied the European style cavalry, and Boernstein would bring him the Germans that would fit the bill. The regiment so far had four well-trained companies under the command of a tough and experienced Hungarian officer. These companies made a glorious showing when they made a devastating charge against a superior rebel force during the battle for Springfield, Missouri, in August 1861.

Missouri was divided between a unionist and secessionist population. When the war began, the battle for Missouri ensued with Union and rebel troops pushing each other back and forth across the state for control. Frémont seemed to have the matter well in hand. Then he overstepped his authority and began to set political policy in the state. President Lincoln removed Frémont from command in Missouri, and the Frémont Hussars found themselves without a home. Boernstein's and von Minden's companies had not yet been assigned to the regiment, and so they, too, found themselves looking for a new regimental assignment.

General David Hunter replaced Frémont in Missouri, but after giving up the ground Frémont had gained, he was replaced by General Henry W. Halleck. Halleck then appointed fifty-six-year-old General Samuel R. Curtis to command the new Military District of Southwest Missouri.

Curtis had graduated from West Point in 1831. Retired from the military, he was serving in the U.S. Congress from Iowa when the war began. He had raised the Second Iowa Regiment in the early months of the war and later was promoted to brigadier general. Assigned to General Frémont's headquarter in St. Louis, Curtis supervised military activities in and around the city.

In the latter months of 1861, military authorities observed that there were several independent companies of Federal cavalry being formed in the Missouri area that needed to be assigned to a regiment to be effective in the field. The four Iowa and Minnesota German companies were one such unit. In Nebraska City and Omaha in Nebraska Territory, four companies of Federal volunteer cavalry were being formed consisting of volunteers from Nebraska and Iowa. From Osage County in central Missouri came the Osage Independent Mounted Rifles, organized in September. From St. Louis there were the "Irish Dragoons," once a part of the Third Missouri Cavalry. The company's captain was severely wounded and first lieutenant killed during the battle for Springfield. These ten companies were ordered to Benton Barracks Camp of Instruction near St. Louis to form a regiment named the "Curtis Horse" after General Samuel Curtis who, for a short time, was in command of Benton Barracks.

In late December, the Second and Third Companies of Minnesota Cavalry were ordered to Benton Barracks for cavalry training. They still had not received any word as to what regiment they would be assigned. During November and December the weather had been intensely cold in the Northwest, and the Mississippi River had begun to freeze over unusually early. Riverboat travel on the upper Mississippi came to a halt, and the Second and Third Companies were compelled to travel overland to St. Louis. The two companies boarded open lumber wagons with no springs for a torturous ride over rough, frozen roads.

Their first stop was at Red Wing for a cold lunch, and at midnight, supper was taken in Wabasha. There was no stopping for sleep. On the morning of December 24, they had breakfast in Winona and then set out for La Crosse, Wisconsin, where they would cross the river. The troops spent most of the day in La Crosse, catching up on lost sleep and recovering from the murderous wagon ride. Captain Brackett had left Fort Snelling earlier than the rest of the men to travel to Milwaukee in search of a regiment to join. On the twenty-fifth he met the troops in La Crosse with no news of encouragement. At two o'clock in the morning of the twenty-sixth, West's and Brackett's companies boarded rail cars and left for Chicago.

The ride in the cars was much more comfortable. Many of the non-commissioned officers, who had easier access to liquor, spent most of the rail trip getting quite drunk, which was a constant irritation to the rest of the troops. After arriving in Chicago in the evening, Sergeant William McGeorge of the Third Company, who was in a drunken stupor, drew his saber and threatened a guard. McGeorge was subdued and put under watch. During the night he escaped.

The two companies covered the floor of the gentlemen's sitting room in the depot of the Illinois Central Railroad for the night. Not an inch of floor could be seen as the men lay across each other. In the morning of the twenty-seventh, the men once again boarded rail cars, without Sergeant McGeorge, for the final leg of their journey. Because of the extreme cold, the windows in the cars were too frosted over to allow any view of the countryside. Unlike the train ride to Chicago, there was no food or hot coffee available. The next morning the train carrying the exhausted Minnesota cavalry finally arrived at the Mississippi River opposite St. Louis. The troops crossed the river by ferry and then marched five miles to Benton Barracks. They still had no orders for a regimental assignment.

As they entered the training compound, Captain von Minden's First Minnesota Company, who had been at Benton Barracks now for two months, and the First Battery of Minnesota Light Artillery fell into formation to greet the two orphaned companies with cheers. The Second and Third Companies were struck by the condition of the troops there. "The men whom we passed and saw in the camp are the dirtiest set of men I ever saw," Eugene Marshall noted in his diary, ". . . and though we have been traveling night and day and are somewhat exhausted, every one we passed remarked how healthy and clean we looked but prophesied that we would change soon."

Due to the dry ground and lack of snow, dust from the red clay soil covered everything and everyone, officers and enlisted men alike. When it rained, the ground turned to a greasy muck making training exercises a muddy and awkward experience. The new arrivals also discovered that there were no real bathing facilities in the camp.

After a few weeks in camp, Volney T. Hopkins of the Second Minnesota Cavalry Company wrote to the *Mankato Semi-Weekly Record* describing his impression of the camp for the folks back home: "The boys, with few exceptions, are in fine spirits. We find very comfortable quarters in Benton Barracks . . . a very pretty place, situated four miles from the city, and near the fair grounds."[1]

Hopkins's report was quite exaggerated, however, and was intended simply to paint a positive picture for the folks at home. A more accurate account of conditions at Benton Barracks was published in St. Paul's *Pioneer and Democrat* from the letter of a man in the Third Company who signed off only with a symbol of three stars.

> We have a thick, sickly atmosphere again today—you could slice it up like cheese. The number of sick in the several hospitals in this vicinity, it is reported, number nearly six thousand and the deaths average sixty-five per week. Fifteen of our boys started for the hospital this morning. Capt. West has a number of his men in the city hospital with the measles. Captains West and Brackett and Lieutenant Smith are sick, not seriously, but too much so to do duty.
>
> I am at a loss to understand why so many troops are kept in these barracks; true, this is called a "Camp of Instruction," but neither tactics nor army regulations are very strictly observed; the most that men do here is to catch cold and get sick.[2]

Corporal Owen E. Gillen of the Second Company also described a frightful atmosphere to the *Mankato Weekly Independent.*

> This is truly a most execrable place in which to confine a large body of men. The climate is miserable, and such quarters as we have are enough to kill the strongest. I will [provide] a description of our room which will answer for all the rest of the garrison now numbering about 15,000 men. The room is about 100 feet long, 80 feet in width, and 10 high. The bunks, three tiers high, are arranged all around the room. In the center is one large stove in which we burn coal of the meanest possible description. It is so strongly impreg-

nated with sulphur as to effect the lungs and throats of the men—
nearly all of whom cough incessantly. The weather boarding of the
building is put on upright and the cracks are not battened so that
there is a constant draft through them.[3]

In the latter part of January, Marshall wrote, "We have been so
completely impregnated and saturated with coal smoke and gas that
we are all nearly dead."

Disease was the common enemy in the camp. No one was immune
from the variety of illnesses sweeping through the ranks such as colds,
flu, measles, and smallpox. Wagons transporting the sick out of the
camp ran daily. One Michigan regiment, upon its arrival, refused to
occupy the quarters assigned to them and pitched their own tents outside the camp in hopes of a healthier environment. Conditions at the
Camp of Instruction were so demoralizing to the troops that it became
known, as Marshall put it, as the "camp of destruction." The first casualty of the Minnesota cavalry troops was eighteen-year-old Henry
S. Lindsay, bugler of the Third Company, who died on January 26,
1862. The next day, Joshua Steiner of the Second Company died of
measles.

The two unassigned Minnesota companies finally received orders
to be mustered into the regiment of Curtis Horse. The regiment now
had a full complement of twelve companies. The four companies from
Nebraska Territory were designated as Companies A, B, C, and D. The
German companies, formerly the Frémont Hussars, were designated
as Companies E, F, G, and H with Captain von Minden and his troops
as Company G. Captain West's company was designated Company I,
and Captain Brackett's company was now Company K. The Irish Dragoons were designated as Company L, and the Osage Independent
Mounted Rifles became Company M.

Colonel William W. Lowe, age thirty-one, commanded the regiment. Lowe, born in Indiana and raised in Iowa, was an 1853 graduate of West Point, who ranked thirteen in his class. He began his career with the First U.S. Dragoons and shortly after served in the newly
formed Second U.S. Cavalry, garrisoned at various posts in Texas. Before the war, the Second Cavalry was the favorite regiment of Jefferson Davis, then Secretary of War. Commanding the regiment at one
time were Colonel Albert S. Johnston and Lieutenant Colonel Robert

E. Lee who, along with many other officers in the regiment, rose to high ranks in the Confederate army. At the outset of the war, Lowe, one of the few officers in the regiment who remained with the Union, advanced to the rank of captain and, with the reorganized Second Cavalry, was engaged in the battle of Bull Run.

In December 1861, Captain Lowe was promoted to colonel in the volunteer corps and ordered to command an unusual volunteer cavalry regiment to be named the "Curtis Horse." Training the regiment, consisting of the odd mix of companies from Minnesota, Iowa, Missouri, and Nebraska Territory, would prove to be Lowe's most challenging task. His second in command was twenty-nine-year-old Matthewson T. Patrick, now lieutenant colonel, who had been the captain of Company A and who had recruited many of the volunteers of that company in Omaha.

The regiment of Curtis Horse was divided into three battalions of four companies each. The Nebraska companies were designated as the First Battalion, the four German companies as the Second Battalion, and companies I, K, L, and M as the Third Battalion. Captain Boernstein, who organized the German battalion, was appointed major during the initial formation of the regiment in late December and placed in command of the Second Battalion.

Boernstein was a sergeant with the First Iowa Infantry when the war broke out. The First Iowa was engaged in the battle for Springfield, Missouri, in the early months of the war. At the end of his three-month enlistment, Boernstein was mustered out of service. Boernstein was a German nobleman by birth. During his service with the First Iowa, he went by the name Carl Boernstein Schaffer. When General Frémont commissioned him to take charge of a German cavalry battalion from Iowa, including von Minden's Minnesota company, to add to the Frémont Hussars, Schaffer assumed the surname of Boernstein to which his rank and German estate entitled him. From then on he was known as Carl Schaffer de Boernstein.

William Kelsay was appointed major of the First Battalion. Kelsay, thirty-one years old, was first lieutenant of Company A and recruited the Iowa contingent of the company when it was mustered in Omaha. When Captain Patrick was promoted to lieutenant colonel, Kelsay became captain of the company. It was known during the initial stages of the formation of the regiment that Kelsay would be placed in com-

mand of the First Battalion. This was decided before the Second and
Third Minnesota Companies arrived at Benton Barracks.

The appointment of major of the Third Battalion, however, sparked
a great deal of interest. Before West's and Brackett's companies arrived, the remaining company officers in the regiment were already
campaigning for the promotion. After assessing the situation, the men
of Company K felt confident that their captain, Brackett, would get the
nod. Brackett was a quiet and modest man but retained a great deal of
respect from his men. He did little campaigning for the promotion and
felt the decision would be made regardless of his own influence.

On February 1, 1862, it became official. Brackett received the appointment as major and was placed in command of the Third Battalion. Eugene Marshall wrote, "The promotion so disgruntled the other
captains who were senior to Brackett that only the strictness of military discipline prevented an open rupture." Brackett, thirty-five years
old, was senior in age to the rest of the regimental staff officers. Major
Boernstein was the youngest at the age of twenty-six.

Sergeant McGeorge, who escaped from his guards in Chicago, returned to his company at Benton Barracks where he was immediately
demoted to the rank of private by Brackett. But McGeorge, a lawyer,
managed to win favor with Colonel Lowe. He was later promoted to
second lieutenant and appointed as regimental adjutant.

Throughout the month of January, horses were brought into Benton Barracks to be issued to the regiment. Small groups of men would
be sent into St. Louis to obtain what horses were available at the stock-
yards. Often there were few horses to be had. On one typical occasion,
when acquiring horses, thirteen men from Company K went to the
yards for horses and returned with only three. Saddles and other horse
equipment were issued, including blankets, feed bags, lariats, halters,
and bridles with bits often in poor condition.

Disease not only ran high among the soldiers but affected the horses
as well. The local veterinarians and company farriers had their hands
full in trying to keep the horses healthy. One of the methods used in
an attempt to cure horses of disease was to bleed them. However, many
times a horse was found dead after such a procedure. Most of the men
did not know if their horses would be healthy from one day to the next.
Marshall was always concerned about the welfare of the horses: "There
are several of our horses that are lame and sick. The grey horse which

I have selected is sick with the distemper, but though he is badly swelled under the jaw, he eats his ration well."

Weapons were also issued in January and arrived in camp at a trickle like the horses and other equipment. The men were not pleased with what they received for arms. Approximately half the regiment received Hall carbines, which were generally viewed as a poor and unreliable firearm. Some of the troops received the Beals patented Remington revolvers that, over time, were found to be equally untrustworthy. Many of the men received no firearms of any kind. Everyone was issued the old-model, heavy Dragoon sabers known as "wrist breakers," which proved to be their only reliable weapon.

The companies that arrived at Benton Barracks in November and December 1861 were fortunate to receive a fair amount of actual cavalry training as they waited for more companies to fill out the regiment. In addition to hours of saber drill, the volunteers were given a taste of what actual battle would be like. Mounted in various formations, the companies walked, trotted, and galloped their horses at ranks of infantry with fixed bayonets who fired blank volleys at them. The same procedure was performed against artillery as well. This drill helped condition the men and particularly the horses for the sounds, flashes, and smoke that would await them in real battle.

As for the Second and Third Minnesota Companies who arrived later, little quality cavalry training took place at Benton Barracks. Much of their time was occupied with trying to acquire equipment, horses, and arms. Attempts to keep themselves dry, warm, clean, and healthy also consumed much of their time as well as tending to their horses' ailments and standing guard duty at the stables. Occasionally there was saber drill, and when there were enough healthy horses, mounted drill was performed. Just as with their drills at Fort Snelling, the drills were were often led by officers who had little understanding of the cavalry manual in spite of Colonel Lowe's orders that all officers and noncommissioned officers must be proficient with it.

The volunteer soldiers of the Union army were ill prepared for cavalry service from the beginning. These were men from a variety of backgrounds; few of them had ever ridden a horse or had any knowledge of horsemanship. In the North, improved roads made it possible for city dwellers and farmers alike to use wheeled vehicles as a primary means of transportation. The horses issued to the troopers had barely been broken in and many not at all. With unbroken horses and riders who regarded the horse with a novelty-like curiosity, initial mounted training was a dangerous or often comical affair. After only a few weeks of training, the volunteer cavalry was thrust into the field. In the regular U.S. Cavalry, it was believed that a cavalryman was of little real value until he had at least two years of service.

General William T. Sherman was in command of Benton Barracks at this time. Discouraged over his ability to command troops early in the war, Sherman retired to his home in a state of despair and felt he no longer was capable of leading troops into battle. His superiors, still confident in his skills, ordered Sherman to oversee the training of troops at Benton Barracks in order to rebuild his self-confidence. Sherman was popular among the common soldiers for his fair treatment and respect for them. He knew the volunteers needed to be handled more carefully. His treatment of officers, however, was more strict. "A new uniform and a commission counted for much less than at Fort Snelling," Eugene Marshall noted, " . . . and while a private sent to his headquarters with a message was sure of the most courteous treatment, an officer asking for a favor was very likely to be treated to a decided snub."

On one occasion when Company K was engaged in mounted drill on the parade ground, Captain Erwin Shelley, who was now commanding the company after Brackett was promoted, ordered the formation to perform a wheel at a gallop while General Sherman looked on. Many of the horses were without shoes. During the maneuver, the far end of the formation passed over a large patch of ice that scattered the ranks and threw Barzilla Carr and his mount to the ground. Sherman came over to the scene, retrieved Carr's horse, helped him collect his belongings, and assisted the stunned trainee into the saddle. The general then sternly lectured Shelley on the hazards of marching barehoofed horses over icy ground.

The troops took every opportunity they could find to get away from the trials at camp. Often they would travel into town or to a nearby tavern for beer and whiskey. Marshall described one trip out of the camp on a warm day when Captain West's Company I led Shelley's company to a local watering hole:

> As soon as we got outside of the lines, West's Co. started at a gallop and soon left us behind, but as we proceeded we occasionally

overtook a straggler by the side of the road, horse and man both covered with mud. . . . When we arrived at the six mile house, we found the muddiest set of men I ever saw, drawn up in column of fours, drinking beer, and our company was soon wheeled into the same position and were marched up to the door, and beer or whiskey at will was dealt out to the men.[4]

The troops were getting restless and looking for any escape from the wearisome drudgery of camp. Ready or not, they were determined to get into the field or be sent home. Death in battle was now a welcome prospect compared to the disease and despair at Benton Barracks.

# Into the Fight at Last

IT WAS CERTAIN the Curtis Horse would be joining General Curtis in Rolla, Missouri, and begin an offensive to drive the rebels out of the state. During the latter part of January 1862, the troops were anxious to leave the misery of Benton Barracks and get into action even though their training was less than adequate and they had few weapons. Generals Halleck and Curtis both made repeated requests to General Sherman for the regiment to be sent into the field. But the requests were denied due to the regiment's lack of horses, lack of arms, and their general lack of training.

Finally on February 7, the regiment was ordered to pack their belongings, saddle their horses, and be ready to march out at a moment's notice, only to be ordered back to the stables and to unsaddle. The next morning they were ordered to saddle and again returned to the stables. Later in the day they saddled once more and finally departed the camp. The regiment marched through St. Louis and halted at the docks on the Mississippi River. The steamboats *Hannibal City, Continental,* and *G.W. Graham* were waiting to be boarded by the three battalions. To the troops, steaming down the Mississippi to join General Curtis farther inland seemed like an odd route to take.

Nonetheless, the men were jubilant with the prospect of finally getting into the war. On the *G.W. Graham,* many of the officers and enlisted men of the Irish Dragoons, Company L, drank whiskey and drew their weapons to celebrate. The festivities turned into a near riot, and several of the most drunken were taken below deck and tied with ropes to prevent them from hurting themselves and others. The Officer of the Day, Lieutenant William Smith of the Minnesota Company I, ordered the guards to run anyone through with their sabers who was caught stealing from the soldiers or drawing a weapon in a drunken celebration.

As night fell, the steamboats were still tied to the banks. The men bedded themselves down on the cabin floors, but they were too excited to sleep. The next morning the soldiers discovered they still had not left the banks of St. Louis, and the ice on the river was thicker than it had been the day before. Word of their destination was finally received. They were to go directly to Fort Henry on the Tennessee River in northern Tennessee. The men were confused, knowing General Curtis was not in Tennessee, but nonetheless were happy to know they were going to get into action.

General Ulysses S. Grant and his troops had captured Fort Henry only three days earlier. The War Department had decided that Curtis had enough troops in Missouri to get the job done. The poorly armed and ill-trained Curtis Horse, the department determined, was more suited for garrison duty at Fort Henry. Grant was now making preparations to move on the Confederate-held Fort Donelson on the Cumberland River just a few miles away. The three steamers carrying the Curtis Horse pulled away from the banks of St. Louis and headed down the Mississippi to the mouth of the Ohio River. After a four-hour stop at Cairo, Illinois, the regiment steamed up the Ohio and stopped briefly at Paducah, Kentucky, near the mouth of the Tennessee.

As they steamed up the Tennessee, the men noticed the river was unusually high for that time of year. Many lowland fields, woodlands, and small buildings were under water along the banks. Trees along the riverbank had begun to send out tufts of green leaves as they were stimulated by the warm river water. The evidence of war was clearly visible as the three steamers traveled down the Mississippi and up the Ohio. Fortified artillery batteries could be seen along the river's edge, and occasionally a small town bearing the scars of a battle received from one side or the other. But on the Tennessee all seemed quiet and peaceful. With budding trees in the dead of winter came a sense of a new beginning for the men.

The steamers reached Fort Henry, and for the first time since leaving St. Louis the regiment was back on land. The fort was on low ground near the river and commanded a good portion of the waterway in both directions. The Curtis Horse made camp outside the fort in a dense forest. The ground there was like a sponge. Water was everywhere, and there were no dry spots on which to pitch a tent. This was not the kind of camp environment the troops had envisioned. To keep their beds dry, the men gathered dry corn stalks and cotton from nearby fields. After camp was fairly well situated, the men found time to tour the fort and see just what it was they would be protecting.

The fort was in poor shape, and the effects of the previous battle were evident everywhere. Pieces of shell and shot and unexploded rounds littered the ground in and around the fort. During the Union attack, gunboats under the command of Commodore Andrew Foote blasted the walls of the fort at nearly point-blank range, heavily damaging the fortifications as well as some of the crude log huts inside. By the looks of things, the Confederate garrison left in a hurry. Artillery pieces, equipment, food, clothing, and personal belongings were scattered everywhere.

Most of the Confederate forces at Fort Henry had fled to Fort Donelson a few miles to the east on the west bank of the Cumberland River. Fort Donelson stood on a high bluff overlooking the river and was heavily fortified. Grant moved his force of fifteen thousand troops into position for an attack on February 13. During the battle he would be reinforced with an additional twelve thousand men. The Confederate troops at the fort were nearly equal in number to Grant's forces.

The fighting halted temporarily on the night of the thirteenth. It had been raining most of the day, and as night fell the rain turned to sleet, the sleet turned to snow, and the temperature dropped to below freezing. Grant's troops were not allowed to light campfires so as not to give away their positions. The Federal troops suffered greatly.

The next day, Commodore Foote moved his gunboats up the Cumberland to attack the fort on the east side as he had done against Fort Henry. However, the Confederate artillery high above the river was too much for the river fleet, and Foote was forced to withdraw. Grant settled in for a siege by land and surrounded the fort.

The Curtis Horse Cavalry remained at Fort Henry while occasionally receiving word of the progress of the battle at Donelson. Day and night they could hear the constant thunder of the artillery dual twelve miles away and eagerly waited for an order to be called into the battle. For a few, an order finally came. Lieutenant Colonel Patrick was ordered to take three companies from the regiment thirty miles up the Tennessee River to destroy a railroad bridge. Patrick took Captains William Haw, von Minden, and West and their Companies F, G, and I for the mission.

The bridge linked the Memphis and Ohio Railroad between Memphis, Tennessee, and Bowing Green, Kentucky, passing by Fort Donelson along the way. The rail line would be a vital source of transportation for the Confederates bringing reinforcement troops and supplies to the garrison at the fort. Patrick and the three companies reached the bridge at daybreak on the morning of February 15. A small group of Confederate pickets were easily driven off, and the bridge was quickly destroyed. The detachment arrived back at Fort Henry at noon on the same day having marched sixty miles in twenty-four hours with only one rest stop. The men and horses were exhausted.

The battle for Fort Donelson continued. Union wounded came into Fort Henry bringing news of hundreds of men killed and wounded. Major Brackett carried dispatches between commanders during the battle and brought back similar news of heavy losses on both sides. The battle pitched back and forth with each side gaining ground and then retreating. On the night of the fifteenth, the temperature dropped again to ten degrees Fahrenheit.

On the sixteenth the Confederate commanders inside Fort Donelson discussed their fate. They realized reinforcements would not arrive while mistakenly believing that Grant had received more troops. The decision to surrender was made, and Grant accepted it unconditionally. The Confederate cavalry commander, Lieutenant Colonel Nathan Bedford Forrest, refused to surrender and led his regiment out of the fort to safety during the night completely undetected. In the years to follow, Forrest would return again and again to haunt Union forces.

After the surrender, fifteen thousand Confederates were taken prisoner. Several artillery pieces, numerous horses, a large quantity of supplies, and thousands of muskets were captured as well. Total casualties on both sides mounted to more than thirty-four hundred killed and wounded. The victory placed Union forces in control of northern Tennessee, and with the help of General Curtis in Missouri, Federal troops now were able to put pressure on the Confederacy from the West. But there was much work yet to be done in Tennessee.

Curtis Horse was assigned to General Lew Wallace's Third Division with Major Kelsay's First Battalion being attached to the Second Brigade. They occupied Fort Heiman on the Kentucky side of the Tennessee River opposite Fort Henry. The remainder of Curtis Horse was attached to the Third Brigade. General Wallace was irritated by Colonel Lowe's repeated requests for more arms and equipment.

The regiment was still in poor shape, and many of the men were without pistols or carbines. In late February, Lowe sent Charles Plummer of the Minnesota Company K on one of several trips to Wallace's headquarters at Fort Donelson with a request for arms. There was little Wallace could do. Equipment for the Union troops in the West was slow in coming and often of poor quality. The troops in the East had a higher priority. Wallace told Plummer to report back to Lowe and tell him that, "He might sit up here and eat his bread and beef and be damned to him." But Plummer was ordered back with more requests.

During the latter part of February and early March, the weather warmed, bringing several days of hard rains. The frozen ground again turned to ankle-deep mud making camp a dismal place. The horses stood at the picket lines in pools of water and often went for days at a time without feed and hay. Eugene Marshall noted in his diary, "About half of the company went out about two miles & brought in as much rye in the straw as we could carry on our horses. We have been without hay five days, & our horses devour it greedily."

Finally the Second and Third Battalions moved to dryer ground about one mile away from the original camp. The move lifted the spirits of the men, but getting there was no easy task. Marshal wrote, "After the order to move was given, there was no rest for anyone until long after dark. All our teams stuck in the mud, & at one time 12 mules were vainly trying to move an empty wagon out of the mud. We all worked & lifted until nearly exhausted."[1] The tents and other equipment were dragged by hand through the mud until they could be loaded into the wagons on firmer ground.

The men occupied much of their time combing the area for forage for the horses and food for themselves. Wild game was sometimes found and on occasion pigs, chickens, and rabbits could be caught on nearby abandoned farms. Staying dry, warm, and healthy was also a day-to-day chore with little success. Disease, thought to be left behind at Benton Barracks, still plagued the ranks. Twenty-six-year-old Danforth Kingsley of Company K became severely ill. Marshall was ordered to take Kingsley to a riverboat that would transport him to a hospital:

> We started out on the ambulance, a four wheeled affair with four seats inside, a most wretched affair for a sick man, & after jolting over about a mile of rough ground by the river. Seeing a boat cross-

ing, I went to where it landed but could not get a chance to go over, but at the third trial I secured a passage & was paddled out amidst brush & logs, etc., & at last arrived there. I took him on my back and carried him through mud & water, & set him down on a munition box, & at last got a passage to the steamer Emerald, which was several rods out owing to the high water.

When I got him on board I went to the Surgeon & asked what I should do with him. He told me to lay him on the floor in the cabin, which I did by the side of two or three wretched looking boys who were evidently wasting away, apparently without care. Again I went to the Surgeon who told me that he would examine him, but though I stayed half an hour he did not go near him. . . . There has been nothing since I have been in the service which so directly touched my feeling as this did, to see boys, almost children, lying there in such a helpless condition.[2]

Kingsley did not return to the regiment. He was discharged in November for disability.

Meanwhile, General Grant was gaining more territory in northern Tennessee. With each of his successes, the troops of Curtis Horse became more confident that the war would be over soon. Daily rumors that the regiment would be converted to infantry or disbanded and all the troops discharged and sent home were welcome news. But all the rumors proved to be false. Life in the cavalry was not what the men expected, and they were eager to go home. Existing in the mud and cold, poorly armed, poorly fed, horses in poor condition, and disease afflicting nearly everyone, greatly tarnished their images of the daring and glamorous cavalryman that so many of the men thought they would become.

The regiment became more active in the countryside surrounding the forts. Separated by companies, the men carried out a variety of duties, which included guarding and escorting prisoners, escorting dispatch riders between commanders, guarding telegraph lines, scouting for enemy forces, and on occasion, capturing Confederate guerrillas or arresting civilian agitators. Still poorly armed, often the men in one company were compelled to borrow pistols or carbines from another company before leaving camp on a patrol. And just as often, the men would take their turns on picket duty armed with nothing more than a saber.

Also, the cavalrymen still had not learned the lessons of proper care of their mounts. While on a march, trained cavalrymen would dismount and walk their horses every so often to conserve the animals' energy. But all too frequently the inexperienced volunteers would gallop or trot their horses over long distances that, combined with a poor diet, left the animals lame and worn out. As a result, the horses were often led on foot after such an ordeal; some collapsed and did not recover.

In March Company K and Company L were ordered to Smithland, Kentucky, near the mouth of the Cumberland River. Their duties primarily were to guard the telegraph lines along several miles of roads. Over a two-and-a-half-month period, the men were occupied with a nearly daily routine of repairing the lines after they had been cut during the night by Confederate sympathizers. Their duties also included guarding telegraph operators, who seemed to have a short life-span, and investigating reports of plots to sabotage Union efforts. Smuggled rebel equipment and weapons were found, and some guerrillas were captured.

During their stay in Kentucky, the men learned that war had divided and confused the people who lived on the fringe between the North and South. Marshall wrote, "One thing appears through the whole, that families have been divided, that brothers & neighbors have been arrayed against each other, that no one knew whom it would be safe to trust, in fact that a perfect reign of terror had been inaugurated throughout the country & that they, as a general thing, hail the Union Army as deliverers rather than invaders & destroyers."[3]

Late in March, the two companies returned to Fort Henry for a brief rest but found conditions at the fort far from being fit for human habitation. Marshall described the scene. "Around the Ft. is now a horrible place, the dead bodies of horses, sheep & cattle, the sediment left by the river, & the accumulated offal of a camp, which appears to have had no police regulations at all, make a conglomeration of smells which is terrible both to health & sense. What men are now in camp are nearly worn out with the extra labor of guarding & taking the prisoners."[4]

The men of Companies K and L now realized that their duties on the telegraph line seemed like a vacation compared to life at the fort; they were eager to return to Smithland. It was there that they could occasionally get some good food from the civilian population and usually found sleeping quarters in a corncrib, a barn, a church, or sometimes in a private home. All of which was much more appealing than a tent in the mud at Fort Henry.

On February 28, Major Kelsay of the First Battalion died of typhoid fever at Fort Heiman and was buried at the fort. His death proved that no one was immune from disease. Major Brackett took temporary charge of Kelsay's command until a replacement could be found. Shortly thereafter Captain Croft of Company B was given command of the four companies. However, his promotion to major would not be made until he proved he was capable of handling the job. Croft's chance came quickly.

Scouts had reported that a rebel force had taken position in and around the town of Paris, Tennessee, for the purpose of enforcing the Confederate military draft law. Croft was ordered to take his four companies in the direction of Paris, located about twenty miles southwest of Fort Heiman. Before getting too close to the town, he would stop and wait for the arrival of the remainder of the regiment and a battery of artillery. On the morning of March 11, the battalion drew near to Paris. Croft was determined to make his mark and bring the regiment its first victory on his own.

The artillery arrived later than morning. The rest of Curtis Horse would not join them until the next day. Captain Croft led his command within two miles of Paris when he encountered rebel pickets who were surprised and quickly captured. The battalion entered the town on a charge but encountered none of the enemy. The rebels, numbering about five hundred, twice the strength of Croft's troops, had positioned themselves on a ridge west of town. Croft brought up the artillery, which began shelling the rebel position, but it was not a full effort. After a short period of firing, Companies A and B charged the ridge. The charge was brought to a halt when the two companies encountered the enemy force, hidden behind fallen timbers, who opened a fierce fire.

After a short skirmish, the Union cavalrymen retreated back to the main body. This time the artillery opened with a more determined effort, which lasted nearly thirty minutes. Finally the rebels were driven off by the shelling, but Croft, realizing he was outnumbered, chose not to pursue. He had avoided a potentially disastrous mistake, but not without loss. The casualties of the First Battalion were four killed, five wounded, and one captured. Captain Bullis, who commanded the artillery battery, died of wounds the next day. Croft was removed from consideration for formal command of the battalion. The position would not be filled until November when Captain Young of Company C was appointed as major of the First Battalion.

# Shiloh and the Siege of Corinth

THE UNION ARMY IN THE WEST picked up more momentum as Grant's Army of the Tennessee moved south along the Tennessee River. West of the Mississippi, General Samuel R. Curtis had defeated a large Confederate force in northern Arkansas. At the Battle of Pea Ridge on March 7 and 8, 1862, Curtis drove the southern threat out of that area. In Tennessee, General Don Carlos Buell began marching his Army of the Ohio south from Nashville to join Grant's forces at Pittsburg Landing on the Tennessee River just a few miles northeast of Corinth, Mississippi. Grant's and Buell's objective was to attack and defeat the Confederate army at Corinth and then drive deep into Mississippi toward Vicksburg.

In late March, Major Brackett was ordered out of Fort Henry with Companies C, I, and M on river transports bound for Savannah in southern Tennessee. Their duties were to assist in the construction of telegraph lines between Grant and Buell, guard the lines over a twenty-five-mile stretch, and keep the roads clear for Buell's approaching troops. Meanwhile the Confederate commander at Corinth, General Albert Sidney Johnston, decided to move his troops toward Pittsburg Landing and attack Grant before Buell could arrive with reinforcements.

Grant had been receiving new, untested troops at Pittsburg Landing. Many of them had very little training, and some had yet to be issued firearms. He and his commanders knew that Confederate forces were approaching. But on the early morning of April 6, Confederate forces swept into Union camps, overpowering and surprising Grant's ill-prepared troops. The bloodiest battle of the war up to that point began between Pittsburg Landing and a small, log Methodist church named "Shiloh." Grant's army was pushed back to the landing in a demoralized state. There they found themselves trapped at the river's edge. The riverboats had been moved to the opposite bank to prevent the panic-stricken troops from crossing.

Brackett's detachment met Buell's troops on the road that same morning and began leading the force of twenty-five thousand men during the day and into the night toward Shiloh. With the situation now critical, the detachment kept the road clear and repaired or constructed bridges along the way. That night, Buell's army crossed the river with fresh troops, doubling the size of the Union force. The next morning, Grant's army, with renewed strength, attacked the weary Confederates and drove them back to Corinth.

Many years after the war, Sergeant Isaac Botsford of Company I wrote a history of the first Minnesota cavalrymen. He always described the actions of the men with heroic pride no matter how large or small the role. When describing the part played by Brackett's detachment in front of Buell's army he wrote, "But who built the telegraph that carried the dispatches which hurried Buell up, and who erected the bridges and repaired the roads which enabled him to reach Pittsburg Landing on that eventful Sunday evening, is told now for the first time."[1] More than thirty-four hundred men died during the battle of Shiloh; more than all the Americans who fell in all the previous American wars combined up to that date.

General Halleck, commanding the armies in the West from his headquarters at St. Louis, felt he was being left out of the glories of victory that Grant, Buell, and Curtis were enjoying. After the battle of Shiloh, Halleck arrived at Pittsburgh Landing and took command of the Army of the Tennessee. Reinforcing the army with more troops, Halleck took Grant's plan of attack in hand and marched in the direction of Corinth in order to finish off the retreating Confederates. His lack of experience in the field proved him to be overly cautious. The army moved toward Corinth at a snail-like pace, covering the twenty-two-mile distance in a month.

Brackett and his detachment of three companies were again placed on escort duty for the telegraph corps during the push for Corinth. The detachment escorted dispatch riders and helped construct telegraph communications between the right and left wings with Halleck's command post in the center of the massive army of nearly one hundred thousand troops. Upon reaching the city, the Union force settled in for a brief siege. Finding no resistance, advance troops stormed in and discovered that the city was completely deserted. The Confederates had quietly evacuated Corinth while offering a false resistance. Halleck's victory was a hollow one.

According to Isaac Botsford, Brackett's detachment was among the advance troops entering the city. It is not completely clear what they did upon their arrival. Presumably, all or part of the detachment was ordered to charge a large mansion, perched on a hill, believed to be a Confederate headquarters. Not a shot was fired as the men of Company I entered the house to make a thorough search. Under one of the beds, the men found a frightened young black servant. While questioning him, they asked who he was, and he answered, "I'm Van Garren's cook!" Seizing the opportunity, the men gained the friendship of the newly freed slave and brought him into the company as their cook. Not knowing his slave name or not satisfied with the name he had, the cavalrymen called him Van Garren. Later, Van became Major Brackett's valet, serving with him for the rest of Brackett's army career. The name Van Garren stayed with him for the rest of his life.

In early June, Brackett's detachment was relieved from duties on the telegraph lines and ordered to scout the countryside west of Corinth. The detachment followed the path of the retreating enemy along the Memphis and Charleston Road. In their wake, the Confederates burned bridges, destroyed large stores of supplies, burned rail cars, disabled locomotives, and tore up the railroad line.

The detachment's mission was productive. Managing to repair two of the locomotives that they found, the cavalrymen returned to Corinth with the two engines, 112 prisoners, and a brass rifled cannon found buried by the rebels. General Halleck, impressed with Brackett's success, named the captured brass piece "Curtis Horse."

# Disaster at Lockridge Mill

WHILE BRACKETT'S DETACHMENT was in southern Tennessee and the remainder of the Third Battalion near Smithland, Kentucky, the rest of the regiment continued to carry out operations from Fort Heiman and Fort Henry. Daily detachments were sent out to investigate rebel and guerrilla activities in the area. On April 10 and 11, Major Boernstein marched the Second Battalion several miles south of Paris to investigate reports of a large quantity of supplies that had been collected and stored for shipment to rebel troops. At Henry Station, ten miles south of Paris, the battalion discovered a large depot filled with hams, flour, bacon, peas, and baled hay, plus several hundred dollars in Confederate money. Wagons were sent for and then loaded with the most useful supplies, particularly the food and hay. The depot with the remaining supplies was then set on fire and completely destroyed.

In early May, the Second Battalion, without Company H, was sent out to scout the area west of Paris, which was still being harassed by rebels. The three companies consisted of 130 men, a weak showing considering each company had begun its service with nearly a hundred men on the roster. But due to the combination of so many men on sick call and a lack of enough serviceable horses, it was rare that any company in the regiment could place more than half of its men in the field at any given time. Often their strength was much less than that. Von Minden's Company G on this patrol consisted of approximately thirty-five men.

On May 6, the three companies, led by Major Boernstein, reached Dresden about twenty miles west of Paris. Boernstein received a report that a large force of Confederate cavalry had moved into his previous camp between Paris and Dresden, cutting off the battalion's route back to headquarters. Knowing he was outnumbered, Boernstein decided to march his command north toward Mayfield, Kentucky, to link up with Union troops there.

In the afternoon they headed to the North Fork of the Obion River where in the evening they made camp near a mill owned by a Mr. Lockridge. Company F was deployed as rear picket guard one-half mile down the road to the south in three lines of pickets crossing the road. Captain William A. Haw fully expected his pickets to be attacked but hoped he could at least prevent the main camp from being surprised. At the main camp, most of the horses were unsaddled, and the men began to prepare their evening meal.

Just after the pickets had been placed in position, the entire force of the Sixth Confederate States Cavalry, accompanied by an independent battalion, attacked. The Confederate commander, Colonel Thomas Claiborne, had learned from local civilians about where Boernstein was headed. Claiborne was confident that a swift attack by his force of more than twelve hundred men would stop Boernstein from being reinforced.

The Federal pickets were driven back to their reserves, who were also quickly driven back. The enemy charged in, capturing nearly all of Company F while most of the rebel force charged through the picket lines heading for the main camp at Lockridge's mill. The officers had left their horses saddled, but for most of the men it was too late. Boernstein ordered the command to fall back across the bridge and form on the other side of the river. But the attack was too swift for most of the men to respond in time.

The fighting continued at close quarters with point-blank shooting and saber duels. Sixty of Boernstein's men managed to cross the river and make their escape. Most of the horses were captured as well as all of the supply wagons. Captain Charles C. Nott of Company E was injured during a fall from his horse but still managed to escape with some of his men. Three of his men were wounded and twenty-one captured. Company F fared the worst. Four men were killed and seven wounded. Captain Haw was wounded four times. After riding his wounded horse at a gallop for about three miles, Haw was captured after he had fallen off his mount, but he survived his wounds. Thirty-two men of Company F were captured. Company G suffered no fatalities. Five of von Minden's men were wounded, including von Minden himself. While the captain was mounted, his horse was shot down, landing on his leg. Von Minden also suffered a light wound to his head. He was captured along with fourteen of his men.

Major Boernstein was also wounded. The grand German nobleman, who hoped some day to return to his estate in Germany, died of his wounds the next day while in captivity. His loss was deeply felt by the German battalion. Claiborne's Confederate troops suffered no serious casualties in their attack.

Corporal John G. Bauer, of von Minden's Company G, was among the Federal wounded. Bauer, twenty-four years old, with a severe wound to his right shoulder, refused the advice of a field surgeon to have his arm amputated. No longer a threat to the Confederates as a soldier and probably not expected to live, Bauer found himself in the home of Mr. Lockridge, owner of the mill where the German troops were routed. The Lockridges were Confederate sympathizers, but Mary Lockridge, the miller's wife, was a Christian lady and had no intention of allowing the badly wounded man to fend for himself.

Bauer remained under the care of Mrs. Lockridge for several weeks. Finally he recovered well enough to travel. Although still weak, Bauer planned his route north. Before he left, Mrs. Lockridge gave the corporal a quilt to keep warm and to cover himself to conceal his uniform until he reached safety. Bauer made his way into northwestern Kentucky where he reached Union forces. After a few more months recovering, Bauer was discharged due to his wound and returned home.

The enlisted men who were captured at Lockridge Mill spent a brief time as prisoners of war in Jackson, Mississippi. On May 15, the men returned to the regiment as paroled prisoners and were assigned to various noncombative duties, such as hospital orderly. The three officers who were captured, Captain Haw, Lieutenant von Vredenburg, and Captain von Minden, were held as prisoners in the South for a much longer period. After spending time in several different prisons in Alabama, Georgia, and Virginia, they were finally paroled in October and exchanged in December 1862.

In June, the paroled enlisted men were ordered back to regular duty. Twenty-two of the men, including six from Company G, refused under the condition that they had not been given certificates as exchanged prisoners. The men were placed under arrest and confined in the guardhouse to be given time to reconsider their decision. But they still refused.

On the morning of the twenty-eighth, Colonel Lowe brought the regiment into formation in front of the guardhouse as the prisoners were brought out. An order of dishonorable discharge was read aloud, and the men were turned out of camp under escort. Most of the men in the regiment sympathized with the actions of their paroled comrades. Their decision not to violate the terms of parole was never held against them by the men they served with.

Meanwhile, Companies K and L returned in June from their "scarecrow duty," as Eugene Marshall described it, on the telegraph lines near Smithland, Kentucky. They were in time to join the regiment on another patrol near Paris. This area in northwestern Tennessee was still being molested by Confederate bands, and Colonel Lowe was determined to bring security to the region. After the defeat at Lockridge Mill, the men were no longer eager to venture into the countryside away from the safety of the forts while understrength and poorly armed. Captain Shelley's Company K managed to maintain most of its men on duty, but as Marshall wrote, their lack of weapons reduced their potential effectiveness:

> We had inspection of arms today. Many of the men have no arms except sabres. It is little short of murder to send us into the country we are going to without better arms. Our revolvers are very poor, & the men who have carbines are little better off than if they had none. A few more were procured today but still not enough. Our company today mustered seventy-eight men for duty, more than any other in the regiment.[1]

Captain Shelley was only able to issue the company two cartridges for revolvers and ten for carbines.

It was learned that the civilian guide, who was with the Second Battalion during its ill-fated patrol in May, had been captured by the rebels and executed. When the regiment entered Paris, home of the man's widow, a collection was taken up from the cavalrymen for her benefit. One dollar was collected from each man and given to the woman. Then a stern warning was issued to the citizens. They were told that the survival of the town depended on the safety of the widow and that regular visits would be made to check on her.

Meanwhile, Major Brackett and his detachment of three companies were still performing duties for Grant and Halleck farther south. While the rest of the regiment conducted patrols in northwestern Tennessee, Brackett's detachment arrived in Humboldt, Tennessee, on June 15 for a new assignment. Brackett was ordered to recruit and train the Second West Tennessee Cavalry. Before doing so, however, the detachment needed to establish its authority in the town. The Confederate flag was brought down from atop one of the hotels and replaced by the Stars and Stripes. Brackett became post commander, and the remaining officers performed duties as provost marshal, recruiting officer, and mustering officer.

Brackett's troops performed other duties in the surrounding area as well. They guarded railroad lines and supply trains for Grant's troops. During several patrols, the detachment captured many rebel soldiers and a large quantity of sugar, tobacco, and other property.

On July 3, Minnesota Governor Alexander Ramsey arrived in Humboldt to visit the troops. Brackett persuaded the governor to stay over and make a Fourth of July address to the troops and civilian community. Union troops posted at nearby Jackson were invited, as well as civilians from the surrounding countryside and neighboring towns. On the Fourth, Ramsey addressed a large crowd for an hour. His speech was impressive. Many years later, Isaac Botsford wrote of his impression of the address: "The writer of this has heard the governor on many occasions, both before and since that date, and is free to say that this was the crowning oratorical effort of his life."[2]

After Ramsey's speech, a lieutenant colonel from a Kansas infantry regiment took the platform to make a second address. According to Botsford, the officer opened his speech with some rather disturbing remarks by saying, "We are going to take all your Negroes, confiscate everything you have got, and burn your buildings." Ramsey was not impressed with what he heard and, with Brackett, left the platform for the major's headquarters. Botsford wrote, "The major was kept busy during the rest of our stay there in trying to convince the citizens that the Kansas colonel did not reflect the general sentiment of the army."

# A New Name for Curtis Horse

IN THE SPRING OF 1862, the War Department in Washington began reorganizing the military in order to strengthen the chain of command and provide more consistency in keeping track of troop movements. One of the changes made was in the designation of the more loosely named units of troops. In mid-June, Colonel Lowe was ordered to rename the regiment of Curtis Horse, preferably assigning it the name of some state. The decision for Lowe was not difficult. General Curtis hailed from Iowa as did Lowe. Companies E, F, and H of the Second Battalion, originally organized by Boernstein as the Frémont Hussars, were from Iowa, and half of the men in each of the four companies of the First Battalion, mustered in Nebraska Territory, were from Iowa. The unit thus became the Fifth Regiment of Iowa Volunteer Cavalry.

On the nineteenth, Captain Shelley received a blank muster roll for his company with the name "5th Iowa Cavalry" attached to it. Shelley refused to fill out the roll, stating he had not been given official notification his company belonged to such a regiment. The men of Company K were highly irritated by the name change, especially because of the name itself. Several of the men in the company convinced Corporal Marshall, known for his writing skills, to draft a petition to be signed by all the men in the company and addressed to Minnesota's Governor Ramsey, requesting their removal from the regiment. Marshall summed up the mood of the troops in a very direct letter.

June 20, 1862
To the Honorable Alexander Ramsey,
Governor of the State of Minnesota:

The undersigned members of Captain Shelley's Company of Minnesota Cavalry; known as Company K, Curtis Horse Regiment, would respectfully represent, that from causes entirely beyond their control, we have been placed in a position in the army of the United States, dishonorable to us as a company and as individuals, and doubly dishonorable to the state of Minnesota, whose honor we are anxious to uphold and sustain. The Curtis Horse Regiment is made up of skeleton companies from several states numbering from fifteen to fifty effective men each, and from the best information within our reach, we believe that the regiment does not number over five hundred effective men at this time. Four companies are now on detached service, leaving eight here. One of these companies has no commissioned officers and no other company here has more than one commissioned officer on duty except our own. We have no means of knowing how many men are on duty at this post, but on details for post guard, our company has for several days furnished one third, the other companies furnishing two thirds.

We have never been fully armed, about thirty of the men having revolvers of a very poor quality, about twenty others having carbines and the remainder only sabres. We have been put on picket guard in the face of the enemy in force with no arms but sabres, and it is an every day occurrence that someone of the men have either to borrow arms or suffer reprimand from the Officer of the Day for want of them. Our regimental field and staff officers, who nearly all belong to one family, have overlooked, if they have not encouraged, conduct on the part of several of the companies which has caused the name of our regiment to be a byword of reproach to the whole army, and we are stigmatized as a band of cowardly horse thieves whose only object is plunder.

To this reputation we have in no way contributed. We have been on detached service several months, stationed with the people of the country and beyond the immediate control of our officers, and we have yet to learn of a single instance in which one of our number has been accused of committing any depredations whatever. And now, when our reputation has become such that our brigade command has been heard to call us horse thieves and jayhawkers, the name of the regiment is to be changed to Fifth Iowa Cavalry, and thereby all distinction of state organization is lost to us.

For these reasons we respectfully ask that the influence of the executive may be exerted to extricate us from the helpless condition in which we are placed. We do not shirk from any of the duties which as soldiers we owe to the country, but we wish to be placed in a position where our reputation will depend upon our own conduct.[1]

The petition was signed by the entire company with the exception of Captain Shelley. He was not in favor of the petition but did not forbid sending the document. In fact, the letter was conveyed to the governor without Shelley's knowledge. Corporals Jasper Brown and Daniel McKean were being discharged for disability and sent home. The letter was given to the two men who promptly forwarded it to the governor upon their arrival in Minnesota. It nearly missed Ramsey.

Ramsey received the petition just prior to his departure for Tennessee, where he would deliver his Fourth of July address at Humboldt while visiting Brackett's detachment there. Ramsey believed that the concerns of Company K were a military matter. He dispatched the letter to General Halleck who in turn, as luck would have it, sent it to Colonel Lowe. Lowe became heated by what he read but was not unforgiving. He was not about to grant any great favors to the company but dismissed the matter without reprisal. It seems Captain Shelley was Lowe's favorite company officer and, after all, Company K maintained the most men on duty. Shelley nervously tried to determine who instigated the petition but without success.

It is not known how Major Brackett and his detachment at Humboldt felt about the name change. Brackett was always diplomatic. Sometime after the war, Brackett wrote an abbreviated history of the first companies of Minnesota Cavalry as sort of a reference guide for Lowe's writings. Referring to the regiment's name change, he wrote, "I can find no record of any order changing the name nor do I recollect any such order."

Shelley, embarrassed by the company petition and unable to pin responsibility on anyone, was determined to re-establish his authority. Harsh punishments were frequently handed down for minor offenses. Shelley's actions were often influenced by brandy, which he indulged in frequently. His first lieutenant, Mortimer Neely, was famous for his whiskey consumption. Shelley's drinking forced him to wear "huge green goggles" during the day to protect his bloodshot eyes from the sun. However, his excessive behavior and, no doubt, prior experience in service with the dragoons may have been a major factor for the company being the cleanest and healthiest in the regiment. Shelley would often order the men out for dress parade at the oddest of times, sometimes while on patrol, and then proceed to lecture them about the importance of cleanliness.

During the months of June, July, and August, the newly named Fifth Iowa Cavalry made its base of operations at Fort Heiman on the west side of the Tennessee River opposite Fort Henry. The adjacent Henry County, with Paris in the center, was believed to be one of the most prosecessionist counties in the state. The regiment continued to patrol the county as they investigated rebel activity and made Federal authority known.

The question of what to do with contrabands kept the men active from time to time. Before June, the troops were under orders to turn runaway slaves away from camp and, if possible, return them to their owners. But these orders were mostly ignored. Usually, blacks coming near the picket guards were given directions on what routes to take to make their way farther north. Often the pickets would look the other way as runaways crossed the lines into camp. Many of them worked as cooks until a less-than-sympathetic officer ordered them out.

When an owner approached the camp looking for his escaped slaves, the soldiers found a great deal of fun playing keep-away. After the man entered the camp and found his slaves, he would not be allowed to leave without a pass from the commanding officer. Colonel Lowe would issue a pass to the citizen who would then present the pass to the guard. As the man passed out of camp with the slaves following, they would be stopped by the guard's saber, keeping them inside the camp. The guard would explain that the pass to leave camp was only for the bearer and did not include anyone else. When the man demanded to be allowed to return to camp to obtain a pass for his slaves, he was refused entrance, leaving him furious.

In June, Lowe received a message from General Grant's adjutant stating that, by an act of Congress, slaves would not be returned to their owners. However, the contrabands still would not be allowed into the camps. Lowe chose to bend the orders slightly. He allowed his men to keep in camp only those blacks working as cooks or performing other important tasks.

Near the end of August, the regiment received reports of a Confederate build up near Fort Donelson and that an attack on the fort was expected. The Fifth Iowa crossed the river and made camp on their old site at Fort Henry to prepare. The Minnesota Company G, without von Minden who was still in captivity, was sent to Fort Donelson ahead of the regiment to render assistance if needed. Confederate cavalry numbering more than three hundred, supported by more than four hundred infantry and one artillery piece, formed near the fort to launch an attack.

On the twenty-fifth, the southern cavalry attacked the outer entrenchments but were repulsed by elements of the Seventy-first Ohio Infantry. The southern infantry and artillery were not brought into the skirmish as the attack force retreated from the area. During the engagement, Union troops entered the nearby town of Dover, already damaged from the first battle of Fort Donelson, and set fire to the small community to prevent the rebels from using it for protection. Nearly the entire town was destroyed.

The Fifth Iowa arrived shortly after the shooting had ended. The next morning, Lowe and Lieutenant Colonel Patrick led the regiment out of camp in pursuit of the Confederates. The First Battalion took the advance as the remaining troops brought up the rear accompanied by infantry and a ten-pound gun. Unknown to Lowe and Patrick, a blunder in communication between Shelley and the colonel's orderly delayed the second half of the command for two hours. After a six-mile march, Lowe's advance encountered enemy pickets at the Cumberland Iron Works and drove them back.

Believing the rest of the command was close behind, Lowe ordered Companies B and D to dismount and deploy as skirmishers. The skirmishers encountered more infantry and the enemy's only field piece, which began firing on them. Lowe ordered Company B to mount and charge the gun, which was done successfully. Then the advance encountered the main body of Confederate infantry, posted in the cellars of burned houses and among the ruins of the iron works. Patrick galloped to the rear to bring up the remainder of the regiment, the infantry, and artillery. But to his shock, he did not reach the reinforcements until he had traveled nearly the entire route back to the fort, where he found the rest of the command just starting out.

The short-lived expedition was a repeat of Captain Croft's ill-fated attempt at Paris in March, only worse. Patrick was soon followed by Lowe with his advance troops in tow and badly beaten. Lowe's losses were four men killed, fourteen wounded, and eleven captured. Most of Company B's horses were lost as well. Colonel Lowe returned to Fort Donelson with his command and his pride barely intact.

# Recapture of Clarksville

COLONEL LOWE now commanded Forts Heiman, Henry, and Donelson, with the bulk of his troops at Donelson. On August 29, Brackett's detachment of companies C, I, and M rejoined the rest of the Fifth Iowa at Fort Donelson. This brought the regiment together again for the first time in six months. At Fort Donelson, Lowe's garrison consisted of parts of the Thirteenth Wisconsin, Eleventh Illinois, and Seventy-first Ohio Infantry Regiments as well as Flood's and Stenbeck's Batteries of artillery and the Fifth Iowa Cavalry.

It was known that the town of Clarksville, Tennessee, was a sanctuary for Confederate and guerrilla bands and their supplies. Clarksville, approximately twenty-eight miles east of Fort Donelson, was a launching point for raids into Kentucky, and it was certain that the force that attacked Fort Donelson was from there. This river community, split between a strong secessionist and pro-Union population, had already changed hands between northern and southern armies in the past. The last exchange took place when the Seventy-first Ohio surrendered the town to the Confederates.

Lowe was under orders to use his command to chase the enemy from Clarksville and recapture the town. On September 5, Lowe marched his expedition, numbering more than one thousand troops, across the Cumberland River and made camp on the east side. Marshall wrote, "This soldiering is a reckless, daredevil kind of life, full of laughable episodes & hairbreadth escapes. The river where we forded was about two feet deep with a swift current & sandy bottom. It was truly laughable to see men & horses floundering along through the sand."[1]

The next morning the expedition started for Clarksville. The Fifth Iowa took the advance, as cavalry usually did, with one company on the point. A short distance along the road, the leading cavalrymen encountered enemy pickets who opened fire at close range, killing one horse and wounding another. The advance broke and stampeded back to the regiment only to be stopped by Company K, who blocked the road to prevent further chaos. Companies E, H, and K were then sent forward to engage the enemy pickets. They succeeded in driving the enemy back seven miles. Afterward the command made camp for another night, knowing the next day would bring the battle for Clarksville.

At daybreak the Union forces again took up their line of march, encountering Confederate pickets after two miles. The pickets retreated to their reserves as Company K was brought to the front, and the infantry deployed as skirmishers in the cornfields and woods on either side of the road. As Lowe's troops pressed forward the enemy retreated, stopping to fire a volley, then retreating again.

The Union troops discovered the main body of Confederate forces positioned behind breastworks constructed of logs and fence rails on the opposite side of a plantation. Lowe brought up the artillery and opened with a bombardment that lasted for a half hour.

Lowe again moved forward in line of battle until he was met by a flag of truce. The Confederates asked for a brief period to bury their dead, but Lowe refused. Instead he ordered Patrick to take a portion of the cavalry in advance to save the bridge that crossed the Red River, giving access to Clarksville. Patrick's troops drove the enemy's demolition crew from the bridge before they could destroy it. Then the artillery was again brought up to disperse the remainder of the resistance.

Because of the lack of wholesome food, the men in Company K indulged themselves in things that they would not normally have done during a battle. Marshall recalled passing through a peach orchard as the company advanced against the rebel breastworks: "It was curious to see men advancing upon an enemy & expecting every minute to [be] fired upon, stop and fill their saddle bags with peaches, but so it was. Hardly a man could be seen who had not his hands full of fruit."[2]

Lowe's troops entered Clarksville with relative ease as the Confederates fled through town, escaping into the countryside. Several blacks met the Union troops and reported that several of the town's citizens, dressed in Confederate uniforms, had returned to their homes during the retreat and changed their clothes. As the northern troops entered the town, color-bearers would point to the Stars and Stripes and ask a citizen, "How do you like the looks of that flag?" Usually the answer was, "I don't like it at all."

During the battle, the Confederates lost seventeen killed and forty to fifty wounded; the Union losses were light. After taking control of the town, Lowe's troops discovered a large store of supplies left behind by the rebels. The northern soldiers burned a thousand bales of hay and more than 250 boxes of commissary stores. Another three wagons loaded with Confederate supplies were taken back to Fort Donelson along with several prisoners. Many families loyal to the Union were also evacuated from the town.

Colonel Lowe tolerated the vengeful behavior the troops exhibited against the Tennessee town. The men looted businesses and homes, took horses from nearby pastures, and carried off as much forage and food as they could manage. The Confederate command in Richmond, Virginia, learned of the actions of the Union troops in Clarksville. As a result, Lowe was branded as an outlaw. An order to the Confederate troops in the field stated that if Lowe were captured he would be kept in close confinement and not be allowed the usual courtesies extended to imprisoned Federal officers.

After a week in Clarksville, Lowe's command returned to the forts on the Cumberland and Tennessee Rivers. The Fifth Iowa, once again at Fort Heiman, resumed its patrols against guerrilla activity in west Tennessee. Some of the officers picked up where they left off as well.

In Company K, the officers pushed the men to their limits of tolerance. The list of officers who got drunk while on duty kept growing. All the commissioned officers as well as four of the six sergeants were on the list. Lieutenant Neely would often send out details to pick up whiskey at nearby distilleries. If the detail drank any of the liquor before returning, Neely responded with a heavy hand.

The officers were becoming less tolerant of escaped slaves in camp as well. One morning while Company K was having breakfast, Captain Shelley, in a extremely drunken state, ordered the men immediately to saddle and mount their horses. He scattered the remaining food on the ground and forced the men to remain mounted for an hour as he grumbled disparagingly about the blacks in camp. A few days later, Shelley ordered that any noncommissioned officer who gave aid and comfort to any black person would be reduced in rank.

Corporal Marshall was furious with Shelley's behavior. "Hell has no depths sufficient to punish such contemptible meanness," he wrote. A few days earlier Marshall had described in his diary his impression of the blacks. He noticed that some of the slaves he saw in the towns and on farms were light skinned and often were barely recognizable as blacks: "The race held in slavery here are not all black, they are not all stupid, they know & feel the degradation of their position, & they know that sooner or later this war must inure to their benefit, & they run away from their owners in droves. They are our cooks, our teamsters, etc. They do our menial work & do it well, satisfied with what they receive."[3]

In late October, Lieutenant August Matthaus led Minnesota Company G in advance of infantry and artillery on a march to the town of Waverly, Tennessee. This small community, due south of Fort Donelson, was believed to be the headquarters of Confederate Colonel T. A. Napier. The small Union force of 175 men was under the command of a Major Brott of the Eighty-third Illinois. The troops first passed through the town of White Oaks where every house and building was searched for weapons. As a result two guerrillas were captured.

Five miles from Waverly, the expedition encountered rebel pickets. For most of the day the rebels were driven back by the infantry and artillery until the running skirmish ended at sunset one mile from town. During the night the Union officers determined that they were being led into a much larger enemy force and that any further advance would not be wise.

The next day, the expedition began its march back to the fort with Matthaus's cavalry split between the advance and rear guards. While the Union forces were making a brief stop for water, rebel troops, all mounted, emerged from the woods behind the column and opened fire. As the enemy charged, Matthaus maneuvered his cavalry to the rear to stall the charge until the artillery and infantry could get into position. In his report, Matthaus described the action: "The enemy still came dashing on in great numbers whooping and hollering and at the same time pouring buck shot amongst us like a hail storm. The infantry were now in line and ready to receive them. The first volley of musket balls silenced their whooping & the second fetched them to a halt."[4] As the Confederates retreated, Company G charged. Matthaus, still referring to the company as the First Minnesota Cavalry, stated, "The First Minnesota now charged over the battle field taking seven prisoners; two of them being surgeons. On examination one of the surgeons stated that the enemy was three hundred & fifty strong all mounted, but we were afterwards reliably informed that they were seven hundred strong."[5]

In November, under a flag of truce, Major Brackett went into the camp of Confederate commanders Colonel Thomas G. Woodward and Colonel Napier to negotiate a prisoner exchange. Woodward was the commander who had led the attack against Fort Donelson the previous September, defeated the Fifth Iowa at the Cumberland Iron Works, and was defeated at Clarksville by Lowe's troops. After five days in the camp, Brackett worked out an agreeable exchange. Woodward and Napier probably wanted to relieve themselves of prisoners so they could prepare for what was to come in the following month.

In December, Woodward and Napier joined General Nathan Bedford Forrest on a raid into western Tennessee. Forrest's command swept into the region and defeated the Union forces, capturing Union supplies, destroying bridges and railroads, and generally creating a great deal of havoc against General Grant's supply lines. The raid encompassed most of the area that the Fifth Iowa had patrolled during the previous months. On the last leg of the raid, Forrest was cut off and nearly captured. But the crafty self-made cavalry leader outwitted the Federals and escaped across the Tennessee River with his command intact.

The Fifth Iowa was held in reserve as a defensive measure during the raid and was never brought into action. Lowe's troops believed their commander was a coward for not wanting to risk the regiment in a battle. Later, Lowe proved to his officers that his orders were to make themselves visible but not to initiate contact with Forrest's army. The regiment kept up patrols along the west side of the Tennessee River with little rest. Often the men slept in their saddles as they marched.

As the cold-weather months approached, the cavalrymen were occupied with building huts for winter quarters at Fort Heiman. Small, crude buildings of various sizes and shapes were constructed from materials scavenged from the ruins of buildings in the surrounding countryside. Stoves were made in every conceivable fashion. Few of the men expected to be at this place at the close of 1862. As the year passed, the volunteers fully expected the war to come to an end soon. But with the determination of Confederate forces in the West and the Union's Army of the Potomac unable to gain any ground in the East, the end of the war became more distant.

On December 5, the troops were pleased by the arrival of 250 Sharps carbines. The War Department, however, reported sending 330 Sharps to the Fifth Iowa. These highly sought after firearms, superior to the Hall carbine, were a welcome addition to the regiment. However, after they were issued, there were still some men with no firearms of any kind. That same evening, six inches of snow fell overnight.

# Attack on Dover · Von Minden Captured Again

THE NEW YEAR entered quietly as the Fifth Iowa occupied Fort Heiman. By mid-January 1863, eighteen inches of snow covered the ground in northern Tennessee. Still the regiment carried out its daily routine of garrison duty. Eugene Marshall described a typical day in detail in his diary.

At daylight in the morning the chief bugler of the regt. sounds the assembly of the buglers. About five minutes afterwards all the buglers, some five or six, get together in front of head quarters & sound reveille, which consists of three distinct calls occupying ten or fifteen minutes, by which time all the men are expected to be in line in front of their quarters & answer to roll call. Then another call, & we feed & clean horses & get breakfast. At seven the bugler blows sick call, then the sick, lame, & lazy go to the hospital for their regular allowance of physic for the day. At eight comes guard mount, when the regular post guards are relieved for the next twenty-four hours. This is a formal military parade.

After guard mount the bugler sounds water call, & we water our horses. At noon there is another flourish of bugles & another roll call. At four o'clock water & feed call again, at sunset dress parade & roll call, which we call "retreat." At eight o'clock in the evening, another flourish of bugles & Tattoo roll call. Half an hour after, the bugle sounds lights out, technically "Taps," & the day's work is done. At Tattoo the stable guard is relieved; it consists of a Corporal & three privates who have charge of the stables & horses for twenty-four hours. This is the regular & inevitable routine of the day, but this is not all we have: fatigued details handling forage & quartermaster stores, loading & unloading commissary, etc.

Again, every company takes its turn to furnish a picket guard whose duty it is to guard all the approaches to camp at a distance of two to four miles out. These stay out for twenty-four hours, one third standing guard at a time, all with their horses saddled & bridled, & their arms on.[1]

Company G carried out the same day-to-day schedule while they provided the only cavalry troops at Fort Donelson. Captain von Minden had returned to the regiment in October after spending more than five months as a prisoner of war. In December he regained command of Company G. In the early morning of February 3, von Minden and twenty-eight of his company marched along the west bank of the Cumberland River, passing by the Cumberland Iron Works.

It was known that a large body of Confederate forces might be traveling in the direction of the fort. Von Minden's small patrol was on the lookout for enemy activity but had no intention of getting too close to them. The patrol stopped to take refuge in a few houses to warm themselves. Shortly thereafter, to their surprise, the houses were surrounded by Confederate troops from General Forrest's command. Von Minden's return to the Fifth Iowa was short-lived as he found his luck had quickly run out a second time. The entire patrol was captured without a struggle.

Von Minden had stumbled onto a rebel force about six to seven thousand strong under the commands of General Joseph Wheeler, General John Wharton, and Forrest. The combined force was heading for Dover where it would make its attack. Capturing the town would certainly put Fort Donelson at risk as well and, if captured, would give the Confederates a renewed foothold in northern Tennessee. The ruins of Dover were garrisoned only by the Eighty-third Illinois and a few pieces of artillery all commanded by Colonel Abner C. Harding, a seemingly poor match for the superior Confederate forces.

The three Southern generals requested the immediate surrender of Dover. But Harding refused, prompting the Confederates to begin an artillery bombardment from higher ground. The rebel commanders planned for a combined assault against the Union breastworks after the artillery finished its work. But Forrest started prematurely as he charged his cavalry against the defenses. Harding's infantry and artillery stopped the charge, inflicting heavy losses on Forrest's troops. Wheeler and Wharton also made attacks against the garrison with similar results as the fighting continued at close quarters. The Union artillery fired from pointblank range. Just in time, Union gunboats appeared on the Cumberland River and began firing on the Confederate attackers, inflicting heavy damage.

Just after the Confederates began their assault, word of the attack reached the garrison at Fort Heiman. The troops there could hear the cannon fire from the battle as they moved quickly across the Tennessee on barges. The Fifth Iowa took the lead toward Fort Donelson, followed by infantry of the Thirteenth Wisconsin and Seventy-first Ohio as well as Stenbeck's Battery. At Dover, the Confederate commanders again asked Harding to surrender, declaring that they had not yet used all of their troops in the attack. The statement was a bluff. Although nearly out of ammunition, Harding still refused to surrender.

After assessing their losses and learning about the approach of Union reinforcements, the three southern generals called off the attack and began their retreat. As the evening grew dark and a full moon rose in the sky, an advance company of the Fifth Iowa unexpectedly approached the rear guard of the retreating Confederates and was fired upon. The cavalry was brought up into a column of squadrons with a portion of Company K on the left as skirmishers. As the column advanced, the rebels retreated further, leaving only their campfires behind.

The Fifth Iowa and the rest of the northern troops entered Dover at about 3:00 A.M. finding death and destruction everywhere. Colonel Harding estimated the Confederate losses at 150 killed, 600 wounded, and 105 prisoners taken. He placed his own losses at only thirteen killed, fifty-one wounded, and forty-six captured. Most of the Union captured were von Minden and his men. Harding's garrison at Dover during the attack consisted of only about seven hundred men. Marshall wrote in his diary, "The 83rd Ill. & Flood's battery have made for themselves in this one fight a most splendid reputation."

The next day, the captured enlisted men of von Minden's company along with the other prisoners taken at Dover were paroled by the Confederates. The retreating southern force was short on food and supplies and did not want to be burdened with prisoners. Two weeks later, the paroled men were ordered back to duty by Union officials claiming the former prisoners were not paroled according to regulations. The prisoners had not been taken to an official prisoner exchange site and had not been paroled through proper channels. Unlike the paroled men who were captured at Lockridge Mill, these men went back to duty willingly.

The Fifth Iowa returned to Fort Heiman on the west bank of the Tennessee, only to move again in a month. The Union army believed Fort Donelson was of great value for its location while forts Heiman and Henry were no longer worth garrisoning. On the morning of March 6, the troops left Fort Heiman, crossed over to Fort Henry, and on the eighth marched to Fort Donelson. As they proceeded toward their new camp, behind them they could see the fires at the two forts on the Tennessee River as their old winter quarters burned. The troops had become comfortable in their self-made shanties at Fort Heiman. Now at their new quarters outside Fort Donelson, conditions became cramped as they packed seventeen men into each of the old condemned Sibley tents.

General Grant in Mississippi had opposed the abandonment of the two posts on the Tennessee. He believed the occupation of the forts was vital for the protection of his supply lines and keeping guerrilla and Confederate activity in western Tennessee in check. Grant immediately regarrisoned Fort Heiman. Among the new troops sent to that post, now in ruins, was the Third Minnesota Infantry.

The Third Minnesota had surrendered to General Forrest at Murfreesboro, Tennessee, in July of the previous year. The paroled regiment returned to Minnesota in time to take part in the Dakota War, playing a key role in the battle of Wood Lake, which brought an end to the fighting in September. During the conflict, the Minnesota men of the Fifth Iowa were in anguish, particularly the men of Company I whose homes were closest to the struggle. Most of the officers applied for transfers to Minnesota, and many men threatened to desert and return home to fight. But the transfer requests were denied, and as reassuring news continued to reach them, the men became more content.

When the Minnesota cavalrymen learned of the arrival of the Third Minnesota, they made several trips to Fort Heiman to visit with their brothers in the infantry, eager for news from home. Away from home for more than a year and feeling helpless to do anything about the troubles in Minnesota, the troopers were obviously concerned for the safety of their families and looked for more reassurance that all was well.

As spring approached, the Fifth Iowa continued the duties it had been engaged in for most of the winter. Split up into battalions and often by companies, the regiment guarded telegraph lines, prisoners, and supply wagons. Hundreds of miles were put on the horses as the troops combed the surrounding territory on daily patrols. More guerrillas were captured along with their supplies. Small skirmishes against bushwhackers were common and, at times, running skirmishes with Confederate troops ended with any of the possible outcomes. Short expeditions into the near regions of Kentucky were made as well.

What supplies the troops could not obtain from their own stores were foraged from the countryside. Captured enemy provisions as well as food from the civilian population were brought in. But the supply of horses continued to be a major concern for the cavalry. On April 10, Company I brought in eighty-two horses after a long patrol, leaving nothing in the vicinity fit to ride. South, east, and west, the war had devastated many parts of the country. The small world around Fort Donelson was no exception. Marshall wrote, "The war has made a desert of this part of Tennessee. Never a garden, it is now desolate in the extreme. Miserable half starved women & children, old men & cripples make up the mass of what people are left here."[2]

# The Tullahoma Campaign

GENERAL WILLIAM ROSECRANS, in command of the Union Army of the Cumberland in central Tennessee, was charged with the task of driving the Confederates out of the state. His opponent was General Braxton Bragg, who commanded the Confederate Army of the Tennessee. Bragg's army was situated south of Murfreesboro along the Duck River with Shelbyville in the center of their line. He kept the bulk of his supplies to the southwest in Tullahoma.

The Fifth Iowa Cavalry was ordered to join the Army of the Cumberland at Murfreesboro. The regiment by now had gained a reputation for having considerable experience in long-range patrols. That experience would be valuable in the campaign against Bragg. On the night of June 5, two steamers began moving the regiment with its supply wagons across the Cumberland River, the last of the troops crossing the following morning. The regiment first stopped in Clarksville for the night where they found that their reputation there was much less than favorable.

The citizens of Clarksville were still terrified of the Fifth Iowa, remembering the last time the regiment visited them. In a letter to his sister, Eugene Marshall wrote, "Forrest's men call us Lowe's Hell Hounds." The townspeople pleaded with the infantry garrison posted there to protect them from the cavalry. The request was granted solely to calm the locals as the guards were doubled throughout the town. The only thing on the minds of the cavalrymen was that they were finally going to have a chance to see action at the front.

On the tenth the regiment arrived in Nashville to receive more supplies and spend the night. There they expected to be issued shelter tents, but none were found. The next day the regiment reached Murfreesboro. The Fifth Iowa was assigned to the First Brigade of the Second Cavalry Division, Fourteenth Army Corps. Colonel Lowe by now had developed the reputation of being a topnotch commander. In the absence of Colonel Robert H. G. Minty, Lowe was placed in temporary command of the First Brigade.

After surveying some of the other units of cavalry, the men of the Fifth found they were as experienced and as well armed as most. Along with the Fifth Iowa, the First Brigade contained the First Middle Tennessee Cavalry, the Seventh Pennsylvania Cavalry, the Fourth Michigan Cavalry armed with Colt revolving rifles, and the Fourth U.S. Cavalry armed with the much sought after Spencer carbines. The Fifth Iowa was considered to be the best-mounted regiment in the brigade and was known to be the largest regiment in the division with more than eight hundred men on the roll. Still they believed their chances of seeing action was dim. They were experienced in patrol and escort duty and felt that they would be condemned to the same assignments here.

The Fifth found action soon enough. On June 17, just as the men were settling in for the evening, "Boots and Saddles" was sounded. The Fifth Iowa and the Fourth U.S. quickly mounted and trotted out of camp. The two regiments were ordered to investigate a report of enemy activity twenty-five miles to the north near Lebanon, Tennessee. In the morning, after passing through Lebanon, they struck the rebel pickets, pushing them back in a running skirmish for more than ten miles. It was only after the appearance of southern artillery and the realization that the enemy was twice as strong as they were did the pursuing cavalry call off the skirmish and retreat to Murfreesboro. The men and horses were exhausted by the time they reached camp.

In less than forty-eight hours, the two regiments had traveled more than sixty miles, skirmished with the enemy for a day, and stopped only three times for a total of six hours of sleep. "I believe that I have marched further in the same number of hours but never with so little sleep, feed, & rest," Marshall wrote. "The trip was the hardest we have ever had." During the skirmish, the Union cavalrymen paused long enough in their pursuit to graze the horses in a field of clover and then retire to the woods for two hours of sleep. After the short rest, they again took up their line of battle. A year in the field had taught the northern volunteers the importance of horse care, and frequent contact with the enemy no longer raised the men to the level of excitement that they experienced in the beginning.

On June 23, the Union troops knew a major battle was imminent. Marshall, promoted to sergeant five days earlier, made note of the preparations: "We are [ready] to move. Every man was ordered to take sixty rounds of carbine cartridges & forty of pistol cartridges. We have the pistol cartridges, but thus far it is impossible to get a full supply of carbine cartridges."[1]

The next day General Rosecrans began a combined and well-coordinated offensive against the Confederate line. Marshall and his men observed the activity:

> All day we saw trains of six mule wagons covering miles of road & moving in every direction. The number which we saw was variously estimated by our men at from one to three thousand. On the Salem pike for six miles was one solid column of moving wagons bringing surplus baggage from Triune to Murfreesboro. All the troops have left Murfreesboro & Triune. There is a general movement forward along the whole line.[2]

As the offensive began, so too did the rain. The torrents of on-again, off-again storms for the next seventeen days turned the landscape and Rosecrans's field of battle into a near swamp. Roads became almost impassable, greatly hindering the Federal offensive. The objective of the Army of the Cumberland was to make its attack through three main passes of the low mountain region. On the left of the line, the bulk of Rosecrans's forces would drive through the well-defended Hoover's Gap and Liberty Gap. The Fifth Iowa with the entire First Brigade of cavalry was charged with drawing the attention of the Confederates to the right in Guy's Gap leading to Shelbyville.

On the twenty-fifth, after two separate unsuccessful forays by the Fourth Michigan and the First Middle Tennessee to make contact with the enemy in the gap, the Fifth Iowa was ordered to make another attempt. Major Brackett led the advance with the Third Battalion dismounted as skirmishers as Lieutenant Colonel Patrick brought up the rest of the regiment with the Fourth Michigan following. The forces soon made contact and drove the enemy pickets back. The regiment closed on the southerners, driving them back more than a mile over rocky ground and through dense cedar thickets. The terrain turned out to be so treacherous that a third of the horses of the Fourth Michigan became disabled. The entire Union advance encountered the same obstacles.

As the Fifth pressed the Confederates in a hotly contested fight, the rest of the brigade attacked the rebel flank. The Confederates retreated through Shelbyville and then made a stand with artillery, which forced the Union brigade to retreat. But the brigade's objective was realized, and Rosecrans's army poured through the passes. Company K of the Fifth took up the rear guard as the brigade withdrew from Guy's Gap. Marshall wrote, "I had hardly got to the rear, Comp. F taking our place, when they opened on us with artillery. The shot flew over our heads in all directions. Only one exploded. This was the end of the affair. We had accomplished everything wished for & more than had been expected."[3]

Bragg's army began an orderly retreat across the Tennessee River, destroying railroad lines and bridges behind it. On the twenty-seventh, General Wheeler brought Confederate cavalry again into Guy's Gap to protect the withdrawal and again Colonel Minty's First Brigade pressed into the narrow pass. The Fifth Iowa, having led the attack two days earlier, protected the rear of the new assault. The southern force made a stand at the approach to Shelbyville after being forced out of the pass by the Fourth U.S. regulars and First Middle Tennessee. Colonel Minty placed artillery on the road and fired a salvo into the defense line. Using the cannon smoke for cover, the Seventh Pennsylvania drew sabers and charged the Confederate artillery and riflemen guarding the approach. The saber charge left the Confederate commanders awestruck and was much written about in postwar memoirs.

The Pennsylvanians routed the defenders and forced Wheeler to withdraw across the Duck River just as General Forrest arrived with more cavalry. But it was too late for Forrest. Wheeler was compelled to destroy the bridge as Federal troops closed in, trapping Forrest on the north side. As usual the quick-thinking commander found a way to escape. Following the rain-swollen river, Forrest discovered a safe place to cross with his command intact.

Rosecrans's offensive was a success. The Union army now had possession of Middle Tennessee as General Bragg settled his weary Confederate troops into Chattanooga, Tennessee. While Rosecrans made plans to attack Chattanooga, the Confederates were being reinforced there by more troops from the east, south, and west, building up a massive army.

During the Tullahoma campaign the Army of the Cumberland captured a sizable number of rebel soldiers. Several hundred Confederate

prisoners alone were taken by Minty's First Brigade during the skirmishes at Guy's Gap and Shelbyville. Union casualties during the offensive were extremely light as they were in Minty's brigade. The Fifth
Iowa alone suffered only two wounded. The Minnesota companies received no casualties.

In his jubilation at the success, Rosecrans was satisfied and did not
immediately press the enemy further. He waited until early September to bring his army into Chattanooga, taking the city practically without bloodshed. But Bragg was not retreating. Rather, he was laying
the foundation for an offensive against Rosecrans. The Confederate
strategy worked. Rosecrans's army was lured south of the city across
the border into Georgia were it was attacked along Chickamauga Creek.
The deadly two-day battle resulted in nearly thirty-five thousand casualties on both sides. The Confederates suffered more losses but won
the battle. Defeated and disorganized, the Union army fled back to
Chattanooga for refuge.

# Long Marches and Hard Charges

AFTER THE TULLAHOMA CAMPAIGN, the Fifth Iowa returned to the vicinity of Murfreesboro. The men were eager to remain with the main body of the Army of the Cumberland on its march to Chattanooga. But they found that their initial misgivings of what their duties would be were about to come true. The well-mounted and now well-armed regiment returned to the routine with which they were most familiar. For three months the inglorious work of tracking down guerrillas and scouting, picket, and escort duty again became daily activities.

More Sharps carbines had been issued to the regiment, and most of the unwanted Remington pistols were replaced by Colt revolvers. Nearly every man now carried both a carbine and pistol. They believed they were too well armed to be reduced to duties in the rear. But guerrilla activity in Middle Tennessee still remained troublesome. Also, Confederate cavalry, who managed to sneak behind the Union front, along with the guerrillas continued to threaten supply lines.

Split up into battalions or by companies, the Fifth Iowa patrolled a large area of the country to the north, east, and south of Murfreesboro. Long-range patrols were made in and around Lebanon, Sparta, Woodbury, McMinnville, Manchester, and Winchester. Many guerrillas were captured by the patrols. The monotonous duties of guarding railroad cars and escorting wagon trains of supplies and hundreds of prisoners taken during the Tullahoma campaign also kept the regiment busy.

In early July the troops had much to cheer about. On July 4, General Grant's troops captured Vicksburg, Mississippi, after a long siege. Vicksburg had been the last Confederate stronghold in the West. One day earlier, the Army of the Potomac, in the East, won a decisive victory over General Robert E. Lee's invading Confederate army in a three-day battle at Gettysburg, Pennsylvania. The battle of Gettysburg proved to be the most costly clash of the war. "Today the bells of the towns are ringing their loudest peals," Marshall wrote in his diary.

"The soldiers are half wild with enthusiasm. It seems that they cannot make noise enough."

With two simultaneous Union victories on opposite war fronts, the troops believed the war could not continue much longer. But they remembered they had these feelings before during the course of the last two years upon learning about northern victories. Again in September their hopes were dashed when they learned of Rosecrans's defeat in the battle of Chickamauga.

Just before the Tullahoma campaign, Captain D. Mortimer West, of the Minnesota Company I, became seriously ill and was confined to the hospital. On June 20 he was discharged for disability. The company was hit hard with disease that left only one-third of the men fit for duty. Lieutenant William Smith was promoted to captain, taking command of the company. But he was disliked by the men. The company was united in signing a petition requesting Smith's resignation, stating they had no confidence in his leadership abilities. But Smith refused as he was supported by his commanding officers. At the end of the year when the regiment was asked to re-enlist, a year before their three-year enlistment ended, Smith realized he could not continue to command troops who had no trust in him. Smith resigned on January 30, 1864.

As for Company K, the men had become more at ease with Captain Shelley and Lieutenant Neely. Although still prone to a good deal of drinking, the two officers were carving a more positive place for themselves in the company. Shelley was increasingly more sociable with the men, and Neely was "gaining a glorious reputation" as the company became a more tightly knit unit. Company K was still the healthiest and largest company in the regiment and, more times than not, was counted on to lead the regiment in battle.

The Minnesota Company G continued to carry on without Captain von Minden. For a second time, the surveyor from St. Paul, who had recruited the First Company of Minnesota Cavalry, was paroled to the Union side. As a paroled prisoner, von Minden was assigned as a topographical engineer to the staff of the Second Cavalry Division, now commanded by General George Crook.

With the many miles the regiment was covering on its patrols, the marches were taking a toll on the horses. Feed and forage was becoming hard to find, and many of the horses were being worn out from the long marches. While some companies were out on patrol, others scoured the countryside for more mounts. Many times the only four-legged animal found fit for cavalry service was a mule. Edible rations for the troops were becoming more scarce as well. Often the only food the men had available to them was hard bread and bad meat. On occasion they filled themselves with fruit found in the lush fertile valleys of southern Tennessee.

Over two years they had learned that being a cavalryman was much different from the glamour and easy life they envisioned when they enlisted. Marshall wrote an accurate description of the work that faced a cavalry soldier:

> The life of a cavalryman in this department is one of continual hard work. When marching or camping with infantry his hours of duty are nearly twice as many as theirs. He must be able to eat & sleep in the saddle & must never be too tired to walk a mile if necessary to procure feed for his horse. [If] the enemy [is] reported to be in any particular locality, he must find out whether they are there or not, must go feeling & pushing around their lines to find out their strength like a man feeling with his fingers in a pile of ashes for coals. He must be ready to mount at the bugle call at any hour of the night or day whether he has eat[en] or slept or not. He must be competent, if his own horse gives out, to catch, mount, & manage the wildest horse or mule . . . even though it were so dark he could not tell a horse from a mule. If his horse falls he must always manage to be on top at the risk in the night of being left behind with his horse on top of him. . . . I have known men to be left behind with a horse lying on him & nobody the wiser for it. . . . In our heavy forced marches many horses give out & fall down by the roadside to die or get up again, as the case may be.[1]

In October, as Rosecrans's Union army lay in Chattanooga, surrounded, cut off from supplies, and barely surviving, President Lincoln named General Grant to command all the Union troops west of the Appalachian Mountains. Grant immediately replaced Rosecrans with General George Thomas, the hero of the battle of Chickamauga who saved the Union army from a more severe defeat. Grant brought in troops from all directions, opened a supply line to the troops in Chattanooga, and made preparations to attack the Confederates. In south-central Tennessee, the pace of activities of the Fifth Iowa began to quicken as well.

A large force of Confederate cavalry, under the command of the twenty-seven-year-old General Wheeler, crossed the Tennessee River from the east, north of Chattanooga, and entered the Sequatchie Valley. Wheeler set out to destroy Federal supplies and transportation destined for the Army of the Cumberland at Chattanooga. General Crook was ordered to stop Wheeler. He gathered what he could of the Second Cavalry Division and any other cavalry he could find, crossed the Tennessee, and began the chase. The Fifth Iowa had been detached from the First Brigade for the last three months and was now en route to Alabama for a new patrol area. Most of the remainder of the First Brigade marched with General Crook.

Upon entering the valley, Wheeler's forces captured an exceptionally large Union wagon train estimated to number between eight hundred and a thousand six-mule wagons heavily loaded with supplies. Short on food, clothing, arms, and horses, Wheeler's troops took the best of the horses and mules, killed the rest, and looted everything else that was usable, including Federal uniforms. A large number of the wagons were then burned. But the raiders could not stay long. Elements of the Federal cavalry attacked Wheeler's rear guard, pushing him west onto the Cumberland Plateau toward McMinnville.

Wheeler, still well ahead of the pursuing Union cavalry, easily captured McMinnville, looting the town. Government stores were destroyed as well as a locomotive, a train of railroad cars, and a bridge. Crook was well outnumbered by Wheeler, but after he linked up with the First Cavalry Division near Murfreesboro, the tide changed. Realizing he was cut off from attacking Murfreesboro, Wheeler turned south and captured Shelbyville, again sacking and plundering the town. Wheeler then split his forces between Shelbyville and Farmington, leaving his rear guard at Wartrace. Beginning October 6, the two divisions of Federal cavalry clashed with the Confederate expedition in a series of attacks and counterattacks often involving saber charges.

Two days earlier, while encamped at Decherd Station east of Winchester, the Fifth Iowa was alerted to the approach of Wheeler's army. On the sixth, the regiment began a march of nearly forty miles, first stopping in Tullahoma where Colonel Lowe learned of the Confederate force in Wartrace. Lowe's troops immediately marched for Wartrace where smoke was seen rising from the town as they approached about two hours before sunset. A brigade of Federal infantry had evacuated the town on railroad cars and met the Fifth Iowa three miles out. The cavalrymen and horses were exhausted from the long march, but the day was not over. The regiment marched into town expecting a fight. The infantry also returned on the cars. Eugene Marshall, in a letter to his father, told of the events involving the Fifth that took place at Wartrace:

> We found the rail road bridge & a stockade Ft. there on fire. Leaving the two regiments [of infantry] & two companies of our regiment at the cars, we moved on & soon heard firing from the front. Our company was ordered forward to support another, but we did not find the enemy where we expected & had to change our line which brought us to the front. I had been riding all day at the rear of the company, but in the changes the rear became the front. We saw the enemy & advanced at a gallop. I was next [to] the Captain & the company behind riding four abreast.
>
> At about fifty yards from the enemy, they fired a full volley, & the bullets flew thick enough about as the Captain suddenly found it convenient to get behind me very fast. I fired my carbine at once & loaded again [and] fired a second time. Just then they fired their second volley, & my horse sprang back at the flash of the enemy's guns, he all most trod upon one of our men who had fallen with a heavy bullet through the head. . . . The whole rebel fire was concentrated upon the part of our line where I was. Within fifteen minutes, four horses & three men had been hit, all of them within twenty feet of me. The rest of our line was hid by thick bushes, consequently was not fired at. We have Sharps carbine[s], which can be loaded & fired very rapidly, & as cartridges grew scarce in my box, I looked around to see if there was any one to support us, & I saw no one except our company, about sixty men. But before we were out of ammunition the enemy concluded to leave, which they did very fast. . . . As a last resort, the enemy emptied their revolvers at us but without effect, as the bullets fell spent about six feet in front of us. They were so thick that I could compare them to nothing but a shower of rain.[2]

It was Henry Perkins, riding next to Marshall, who was struck by a bullet in the forehead during the attack. Perkins died three days later in a hospital in Tullahoma. He was the only reported casualty in the regiment that day. It was learned later that the regiment had attacked a Confederate brigade that could have easily defeated the Fifth Iowa had they realized the difference in numbers. However, the Fifth's attack was so swift, the rebels fled in shock.

The Fifth Iowa joined the Second Division and for the next two days continued to press the Confederate retreat into Alabama toward the Tennessee River. On the ninth, the Confederate rear guard made another stand, and again the Fifth was called upon to make an attack with General Crook at their side. Major Brackett brought up companies H, I, and K for the advance. The enemy was driven to a small stream called Sugar Creek where they stopped to make a stand. Brackett's three advance companies dismounted and pressed ahead on foot with carbine fire across an open field. Then Crook ordered a charge. Companies E, G, and M received the order, drew sabers, brought their horses to a gallop, and charged across the field into the Confederate line, scattering the rebels into the hills. During the charge, Crook reported Confederate losses at ten killed, nine wounded, and seventy taken prisoner. Marshall wrote, "We had pressed them so fast that the rest of the command did not know that we were fighting at all."

Followed by the Fifth Iowa and much of the Second Division, the Seventh Pennsylvania now took the lead and continued to drive the fleeing rebels for forty miles. One old woman standing on the side of the road, when asked by a passing cavalryman how many men she thought were in Crook's force, replied, "La, me. I've looked at youans till my head aches." First Sergeant George W. Northrup of the Fifth Iowa's Company K wrote in a letter to his sister, "Our Cavalry was certainly stretched out an immense distance and took hours to pass."

As night fell before reaching the Tennessee River, Crook, having learned Wheeler was preparing to make a stand at the river, ordered another charge. Marshall described the experience:

Gen. Crook dismounted in a fence corner & sent back to the rear for a fresh horse. Soon he went to the head of column, & in an instant the bugles sounded the gallop, & four of the best regiments in this department were after them with their sabres in their hands. They saw the sabres, heard the thunder of two thousand horses coming at the top of their speed. They were off at the best speed they could make; not a gun was fired, not a man hurt. It was four miles to the Tennessee River, most of the way through the woods.

We kept up the gallop till we saw the river, but a few stragglers mis-
led us in the woods, & we went a mile off the road, & before we could
get right again the last one was over the river.[3]

It seems Sergeant Northrup experienced more action at the river
while the Confederates crossed. In a letter to a pen pal he wrote, "They
were pleased to make a stand at the strong rear guard that Wheeler
had left to detain us, to secure his crossing. . . . I think I was never more
exhausted than when the last charge was made by some Georgia and
Alabama Regiments."[4]

During Crook's ten-day chase across middle Tennessee, Union
troops lost only fourteen men killed and 103 wounded. The Fifth Iowa
lost one man killed at Wartrace and one man slightly wounded in the
charge at Sugar Creek. Wheeler's invasion force suffered heavily. The
estimated losses of the Confederates were no fewer than two thousand
killed, wounded, taken prisoner, or deserted.

During the Confederate retreat, miles of road were found littered
with saddles, boots, guns, and everything conceivable in the way
of plunder. Northern uniforms taken from the wagon train in the
Sequatchie Valley were strewn everywhere. Under orders, some of
Crook's troops shot their prisoners found wearing Federal blue. The
Fifth Iowa simply forced their prisoners, persuaded by the butt of a
gun or a saber blade, to take off the Union uniforms.

Marshall's accounting of two thousand horses in four regiments
making the last charge was probably a close estimate. It would place
each regiment at about 50 percent of their original strength. In fact,
Crook's command as a whole was in much more desperate shape for
horses than those four regiments. Losing horses was Crook's biggest
problem during his pursuit across Tennessee.

The command marched along the Tennessee River, making camp
at Huntsville, Alabama. But there was no time for rest. The Fifth Iowa,
still the strongest regiment, made several patrols within the region in
pursuit of Confederate cavalry. On the night of October 17, the regiment marched from Maysville to Athens. Discovering the enemy had
left the area, they returned to camp the next day, having marched seventy miles in twenty-four hours.

The need for horses and rations for the troops now became a major concern. The horses were in a severely weakened state from long

marches and hard battle. And rations were slow in arriving from the troop's former camp in Tennessee. As a detachment of the Fifth returned to Wartrace for the regimental wagons, Marshall wrote about their situation:

> We have no rations now except what we forage. . . . Our men have taken many horses in the country which were needed in the service, but in very many cases the people came into camp after them, & I notice that those who come for them are mostly young & and good looking women. Probably they send the beauty of the family, relying on the gallantry of the officers for success where a man would fail. We need horses badly, many of the men being dismounted & some riding mules.[5]

The Fifth settled into Maysville for a few weeks for a much-needed rest for both men and horses. After having temporary command of the First Brigade for a second time, Colonel Lowe now commanded the division during General Crook's absence. The First Brigade's headquarters occupied a small brick church. A cemetery became the wagon yard crowded with mules and black teamsters. In a letter to his sister, Marshall described the regiment's usual order of camp:

> Our camp is laid out with the regularity of a city: First, Headquarters, consisting of the hospital & medical tents, the commander's tents, the field & staff officer's tents, the noncommissioned staff, the musicians, orderlies, & servants. Next comes in succession the companies, each occupying two rows of tents with a street between them & cook fires on the left, & beyond them the horses tied to a long rope which is fastened to the trees or stakes. On the right of each company are the officer's tents in a line the whole length of the camp with a street between them & the company tents. Each company has its own ground & is not expected to trespass on that of the next company.[6]

After a long rest and acquiring enough mounts during the months of November and December, the Fifth resumed its old routine. In northern Alabama along the north side of the Tennessee River, picket and scouting duties consumed much of their time, providing an opportunity for the men to socialize with the enemy. While on picket at several river landings, the troops passed the time in conversation with Confederate pickets on the opposite bank. Often, against orders, men from either side crossed over in the middle of the night to trade food, tobacco, or news of the war. Many of the Confederate soldiers took the opportunity to desert, which hundreds of others did all along the river.

The regiment also combed the area for livestock, food, and any other goods that would be useful to the Confederate army. Large numbers of hogs and cattle were taken from farms. Only those farmers who could prove their loyalty to the Union were given payment vouchers for the livestock. On a few occasions, enemy pickets on the south bank of the Tennessee, guarding pens of livestock, would release the animals and drive them into the woods upon sight of the Union cavalrymen on the opposite shore.

Colonel Lowe at Division Headquarters was concerned with the possibility that the Confederates would recross the Tennessee to the west in a flanking maneuver against the division. On the night of November 14, a detachment of the Fifth Iowa arrived at the river near Triana and found two large ferryboats on the south bank under Confederate guard. Sergeant Albert Phelps of Company G, with a few volunteers, crossed the river in canoes and rafts and captured the boats. The men took the boats down river and captured six more before reaching Decatur. Under the threat of enemy artillery, the boats were hauled up a creek and cut into pieces.

As General Grant attacked and defeated Bragg's Confederate army in nearby Chattanooga, the Second Cavalry Division at Huntsville continued to deplete Confederate and guerrilla supply sources in northern Alabama. Sergeant Marshall had keenly observed the effect the war had on the civilian population in northern Tennessee. In Alabama he also saw the state of the people as a bitter one:

> I wish I could say that the women here were what the people of the South have always claimed them to be, but I cannot. To me, the greater part of them are unbearably bold & lack most of the qualities we admire in women. Most of them are pale & sallow, & express great contempt of Yankees, yet a half hours' conversation will bring almost any of them into a sociable frame of mind, even with a Yankee. . . . We see no young or middle aged men anywhere in the country. They are all gone to the war either as conscripts or volunteers. Old men, children, & women are all that are left, & if by chance you see an able bodied man, it is safe to ask him what regiment he belonged to.[7]

Marshall felt isolated as it seemed the regiment was cut off from the rest of the world. In northern Alabama with supply lines stretched to the limits, the only news of the war came from Confederate prisoners or rumors among the Union troops. But the *Mankato Record* still managed to be delivered to the old Blue Earth County Cavalry, Company I. In a letter to the *Record,* Lieutenant John Reed wrote, "The Record comes regular to camp and is received as an old friend. By the way, Friend Wise, don't wait for that machine down there at Rochester to grind you out again, but come down to Davenport and enlist in this, the crack regiment of the Cumberland."[8]

# George W. Northrup

LIKE ALL OF THE MINNESOTA REGIMENTS organized during the war, the first three companies of Minnesota cavalry were comprised largely of early pioneers who came to Minnesota Territory as boys with their families or as adults seeking a new life on the western prairie. In Company K of the Fifth Iowa Cavalry, one young man had defied the usual order of pioneering and built a reputation for himself unsurpassed by most. His name was George W. Northrup.

Northrup was born in New York in 1837. At the age of fifteen he discontinued his own formal education and became a school teacher, believing he could educate himself while teaching. George was an intelligent and ambitious young man who certainly was capable of self-education. But years later he pronounced his regret for leaving school, proclaiming no one should give up the opportunity for a full education. His career as a teacher still did not satisfy his ambitions, and so he made plans to go west to the unsettled territories for adventure.

In 1853, with the consent of his family, the sixteen-year-old Northrup set out for Minnesota Territory. Landing in St. Paul, he found employment in a mercantile and fur-trading establishment where he was able to save enough money for a trip farther west. After acquiring a rifle and revolver, Northrup traveled to Pembina on the Red River just south of the British line, arriving in November. There he was employed by the Protestant mission to teach the Ojibwe, Cree, and Assiniboine children. At the same time Northrup learned the Ojibwe and Dakota languages as well as French.

Farther up the Pembina River, he helped construct a new mission under the watchful eye of wary Sioux, who were always looking for ways to disrupt the progress of the French-speaking mixed bloods and white settlers. The Sioux would become an ever-present adversary of Northrup in the following years, testing his courage on several occasions.

In the region of the Red River, Northrup learned the ways of a hunter, trapper, scout, guide, and wilderness explorer. He consumed as much information as any man could about the region and the peoples who lived there. Also, his love of reading and pursuit of knowledge resulted in a collection of a personal library of more than 150 books, which he kept at a settler's cabin near Fort Abercrombie. Northrup studied mathematics, navigation, and surveying and became well read on ancient and medieval history as well as the current scholarly European authors.

Northrup engaged in several different types of employment in the territory. He mapped out the first stagecoach route from St. Paul to the Red River and escorted the first stagecoach. He guided trappers and miners into the western reaches of the territory, served the U.S. Government as Indian agent, and delivered mail along the Red River by dog sled in the winter. George piloted the first steamboat, named the *Anson Northup* after its owner who was from St. Paul, on the river. The steamer, formerly used on the Mississippi, was dismantled and hauled across country by sled to the Red River where it was reassembled.

In 1860, Northrup accompanied a party of astronomers and naturalists on the steamer to the British territory. The scientists were on an expedition to observe a total eclipse of the sun. The men had heard of Northrup and his exploits but did not realize that he was in their company. Northrup always kept himself clean and proper but dressed in the clothing of the Red River people. In a letter to his family in New York during his second year in the territory, Northrup informed them of his character: "Not wishing to 'brag' any but will say that I have not smoked a pipe of tobacco, or cigar, or chewed a cud of the 'weed' or to swear any although I will say 'devil' once in a while when there is no one around."[1]

In another letter he described his appearance.

I was weighed the other day and weighed 161 pounds, and am in heighth 5 feet and 9 inches in my Moccasons. . . . You would see a person with auburn hair reaching below the shoulders. A blue Hudson's Bay coat of "kapose" with a sort of hood on the back to pull over the head when it is very cold weather, with white moleskin pants, and a red sash around the waist with a large knife in its scabbard stuck in the belt, with a pair of fancy moccasins will complete the description of the aforesaid person.[2]

Aboard the steamer, the scientists found a young man unaffected by six years in the rugged wilderness. Edward E. Eggleston, a writer, accompanied the party of scientists. Eggleston also had heard of Northrup but was surprised by the man he saw in their first meeting. Shortly after the trip, he wrote about that encounter.

> I had heard so much of him as a voyageur, that I expected to meet a stalwart, weather-beaten son of the forest, far advanced in life. Instead of that I found him a boyish looking man of twenty-three with soft beard, and flowing brown hair falling on his shoulders, but pushed back of his ears. His complexion is fresh and ruddy, and so far from having the "brag" that we always associate with the idea of a great hunter, he is modest almost to shyness, though very communicative. His whole bearing is such that you would imagine, but for his frontier dress, that he had been accustomed to a parlor rather than a forest. His language is always proper, frequently elegant, though as unaffected as a child.[3]

In another essay, Eggleston described Northrup from their first contact.

> He was clad in a frontier coat made of a white blanket, and reaching to the knees, with bits of red flannel sewed on instead of the ornamental buttons that belong on the back of a coat. . . . I had supposed Northrup to be a man of forty-five or fifty, and it puzzled me for a long time to understand how so much of adventure could have been put into the life of a youth of twenty-three.
>
> Having communicated my discovery to the rest of the party, we set ourselves to cultivate our new acquaintance, a task which we did not find easy on account of a sensitive and dignified reserve that always characterized him. He did not like to be lionized.
>
> Our great surprise, next to his youth, was his diction. Not only that he did not swear nor use slang like other frontiersmen, but that he spoke in well-chosen words which had a certain aroma of books about them. He was not what we supposed a man of the wilderness ought to be.[4]

Northrup's skills as a guide became widely known. When explorers, miners, hunters, or trappers arrived in St. Paul in search of someone to lead them, they were told to trust no one but George Northrup. He conducted hunting parties as far as the Missouri River and expeditions into northern Wisconsin. Many times he and his party narrowly escaped death at the hands of unfriendly Indians, the unforgiving wilderness, or the elements.

In 1855 he set out on foot on a daring solo expedition from St. Cloud, Minnesota Territory, to the Rocky Mountains. Nearly the entire route would take him through hostile Sioux territory as he pulled his supplies behind him in a handcart, with a dog as his only companion. The unrelenting silence across the open prairie was maddening to the point where he could not bear to hear his own voice. But his journey was cut short as he discovered one morning that his supplies had disappeared. For four days, he lived on raw frogs before he reached a trading post at Big Stone Lake.

From that time on he was known to the Sioux as "The-Man-that-draws-the-Handcart." To everyone else he was known as the "Kit Carson" of the Northwest. Northrup became a legend in his own time. Accounts of his exploits were published in local newspapers. In 1855, Eggleston's story about Northrup entitled "The Man-that-Draws-the-Handcart" was featured in the *New York Daily Tribune,* five years before the two met. In 1894, the story appeared in *Harper's Magazine* and the *St. Paul Pioneer Press.*

At the outbreak of war between the states, Northrup resisted the notion of joining the army, believing a life in the military could not match the excitement and adventure he had experienced in the wilderness. But after the Union defeat at Bull Run and the call for volunteer cavalry in Minnesota, Northrup could not deny his sense of patriotism. He felt cavalry service would be the only duty that would come close to fulfilling his hunger for adventure. In the fall of 1861, the twenty-four-year-old legend joined Brackett's Third Company of Minnesota Cavalry and was immediately elected sergeant.

George found a friend in Eugene Marshall. Their common interest in books and writing provided many long discussions on a variety of topics as they shared quarters. Throughout his time in the army, Northrup corresponded with a young woman from Ohio. He found her name and address in a pair of socks he received from a ladies home relief organization. The two never met, but their letters to each other provided a source of motivation for George during difficult times.

As sergeant, Northrup proved to be an upstanding leader of his men. His legendary status in Minnesota was not forgotten either. During the Dakota War, Governor Ramsey wrote to Northrup personally, suggesting he should return to Minnesota and serve as a scout for the troops fighting the Indians. Ramsey's request was made at the same time he was petitioning Colonel Lowe for the removal of the Minnesota companies from the Fifth Iowa so they, too, could return to defend the state. But Lowe was still irritated by Company K's earlier petition to be removed. His resistance to the request was strengthened still further when Ramsey mistakenly referred to the wrong three companies, the Nebraska/Iowa companies, as "Minnesota Cavalry."

After the Fifth Iowa abandoned Fort Heiman and moved to Fort Donelson, Northrup was leading a small patrol in the vicinity in search of the notorious Jerry Stone and his band of guerrillas. Stone was accused of committing several raids against the Federals and murdering peaceful civilians in the area. Northrup vowed he would be the one to kill or capture Stone. The patrol searched a few houses with no results except for the finding of a bushel or more of cartridges in a hollow log in the woods near one house. After leaving one of the houses, a single horseman came riding down the road in the direction of the patrol and called out to one of the cavalrymen to stop and return to him. The request was ignored, prompting the rider to draw his revolver and fire at the patrol. No one was hit, but the troopers returned fire and started after the attacker.

Three of the troopers fell in a creek while pursuing the man who also fell from his horse in the water. Then Northrup rode up to the guerrilla and demanded his surrender. But the demand was ignored as the man remounted his horse and fled. The soldiers, including Northrup, fired several more shots and continued the chase over rough ground. As Northrup closed in he holstered his pistol and drew his saber. By then, the man was too badly wounded to continue. He stopped and begged for his life. It was Jerry Stone. He had received a round in the hip, another in the leg, and one completely through his body. Stone was taken to a nearby house with the expectation that he would not live much longer. There he was left under the care of a citizen. But Stone held on for a year until he finally recovered and then escaped.

In the fall of 1863, General Crook learned of Northrup's reputation for being a savvy scout. Crook summoned him and put him in charge of nine other specially picked men for an important mission. Northrup was ordered to take his scouts behind rebel lines and gain as much information about them as possible. He was to report in person only to

Crook and General Thomas in Chattanooga. This was the adventure George lived for.

Northrup took his men into the Appalachian Mountains and crossed into North Carolina, deep inside Confederate territory. They lived on the good will of the mountain inhabitants who distanced themselves from the war but in general were loyal to the Union. Also, they found the mountains full of Confederate deserters and civilians escaping Southern conscription. Northrup later reported he could have easily recruited a fully armed regiment in a month, if it were not for the lack of ammunition. When the need arose, Northrup and his men passed themselves off as good Confederates as well.

Never discarding their blue uniforms, the scouts crept into rebel camps, gaining a great deal of information. They found the Confederate army in poor condition and witnessed desertions by the score. The state of the citizens was also hard to ignore. Throughout the region, the men found the population barely surviving as the Confederate army depleted their food supplies.

During one trip back to Federal lines, Northrup and his men captured a Confederate colonel, a sergeant major, and a Louisiana cavalryman. But the colonel had to be killed when he jeopardized the safety of his captors. After several months in many parts of North Carolina, Northrup's zest for danger and adventure became too much for this band of infiltrators. Most of them dropped out of the assignment. When Northrup made his final report to General Thomas, only one of his men had finished the mission with him.

In January 1864, Northrup arrived in Huntsville, Alabama, to rejoin the Fifth Iowa, but the regiment was gone. Most of the regiment had reenlisted and was making its way north for thirty days of "veterans furlough." The Fifth had turned in their mounts and horse equipment at Pulaski, Tennessee. From there the regiment rode boxcars to Nashville where Northrup caught up with his company and filled the men's ears with stories of his adventures. At Nashville, all arms and equipment were turned in and boxed for storage. On January 29, the regiment steamed down the Cumberland River to the Ohio and arrived at Cairo, Illinois, on the thirty-first. From there the companies went their separate ways bound for home.

Just as they had entered the war, the men returned home in the dead of winter. At Cairo, the three Minnesota companies boarded railroad cars. The winter cold went unnoticed as the journey home was no less than glorious. But they were different men now. Two years of war had changed them. They were older beyond their years, confident, tired, and skilled soldiers. And they knew, after thirty days, they would begin again. At that time they would return to the fighting with no false expectations of how much longer the war would linger. But their return was a month away, and all that mattered now was home.

*The recruiter and original captain of the Third Company of Minnesota Cavalry, Major Alfred B. Brackett commanded the Third Battalion of the Fifth Iowa Cavalry.*

*A graduate of West Point, William W. Lowe fought in the first major ground battle of the Civil War before taking command of the Fifth Iowa Cavalry.*

*The recruiter and commander of the First Company of Minnesota Cavalry, the "German Company," Captain Henning von Minden was twice captured in the South.*

*At the headquarters of Brackett's Battalion near Sioux City in May 1865, Van Garren (second from left), Major Brackett (seated on left), Eugene Marshall (seated on right), and others paused for a photographer to record the scene.*

*After serving with the Army of the Potomac in the East, General Alfred Sully led campaigns against the Dakota.*

*George Northrup was a legend in Minnesota. This photo of the young and more dapper Northrup was carried by his good friend Eugene Marshall.*

*Eugene Marshall's extensive war diaries provide a firsthand record of the life of a cavalryman and the history of Brackett's Battalion.*

*This lithograph of Benton Barracks from a camp letterhead portrays a pleasant compound, but it was a miserable winter training camp for Union troops in the West.*

*Major Brackett and his aide, Van Garren, on the right,
at a camp in Dakota Territory in 1864.*

*Captain John A. Reed of Company B,
Brackett's Battalion*

*During the Battle of Killdeer
Mountain, James Edwards
sought revenge for his father's
death at the hands of the
Dakota.*

*Captain Ara Barton of Company D,
Brackett's Battalion*

*In 1906 men of Brackett's Battalion gathered at the old state capitol building in St. Paul for a reunion.*

OPPOSITE:
*This oil painting done by Carl L. Boeckmann in 1910 is an accurate depiction of the battle of Killdeer Mountain on July 28, 1864. The painting hangs in the Minnesota State Capitol.*

*John L. McConnell, shown here in 1941, was the last surviving veteran of Brackett's Battalion. He and his father both served on the Northwestern Indian Expedition of 1864.*

# PART TWO

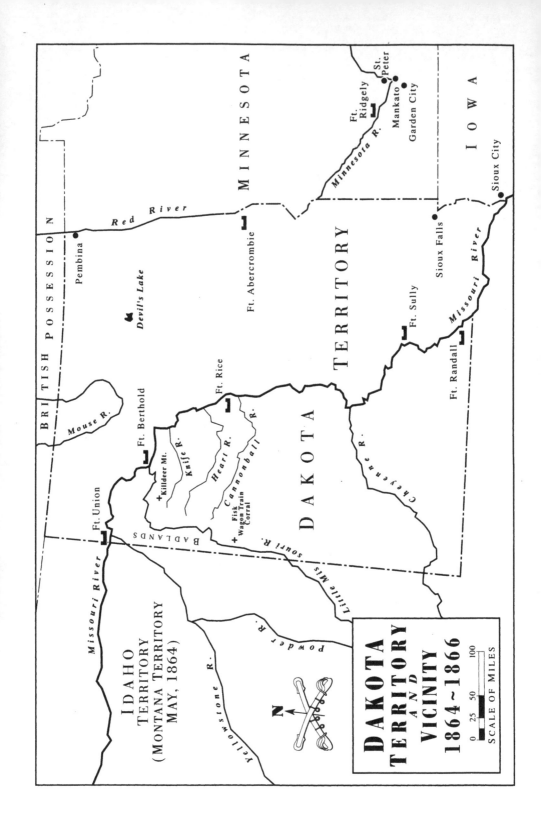

DAKOTA TERRITORY AND VICINITY 1864~1866

SCALE OF MILES

0  25  50    100

# Brackett's Battalion
## and the Northwestern Indian Expedition

DURING THE MONTH OF FEBRUARY 1864, the men of the three companies of Minnesota Cavalry spent time with family and friends, catching up on the home news. Many of them had wives and children. During the soldiers' two-year absence, their families had struggled to get by. The men did what they could while on furlough to prepare their families for another long absence. Some of the cavalrymen returned home earlier with discharges because of disabilities. Some never returned.

Three men were killed in battle or later died from their wounds. But it was disease that inflicted the largest toll on the three companies during the first two years. Nineteen men in all died from disease while sixty-five were discharged for disabilities, mostly from disease. The second company, Company I, suffered the most from disease; eight died and thirty-four were discharged for disabilities. Captain West, Second Lieutenant Nathan Bass, and four of the sergeants were discharged for disabilities.

As the men spent their furloughs at home, Major Brackett used his time for business. Brackett believed that the three companies would be most useful remaining at home, defending the state against the Indian threat. He remembered that Governor Ramsey felt the same way. Ramsey was unsuccessful in his attempt to detach the three companies and bring them back to Minnesota during the Dakota War in 1862. With the companies at home on furlough, Ramsey, now a U.S. Senator, and Brackett saw this as an opportunity to keep the men in the state. General John Pope, commander of the Department of the Northwest, headquartered in Milwaukee, also sought to transfer the three companies to his command for operations against the Sioux in Dakota Territory.

While Pope made his requests to General Halleck in Washington, D.C., Brackett and Senator Ramsey traveled to Washington to make their plea to the War Department in person. Brackett could not have had a better ally than the senator. Ramsey was a skilled politician and possessed a good deal of influence in Washington. The arguments of Pope and Ramsey were convincing despite Halleck's reluctance to break up a veteran regiment. As the cavalrymen began to meet at Fort Snelling at the end of February where they would start for Davenport, Iowa, they received word that they had been transferred out of the Fifth Iowa Cavalry and reassigned to the Department of the Northwest.

The troops reacted to the news with mixed emotions. Many of the men believed, as experienced veterans, they should continue their service in the South and see the war through to the end. Moreover the climate in the South for soldiering had become much more to their liking. However, the Indians in Dakota Territory were still perceived to be a definite threat to Minnesota. Remaining close to home in defense of their state was a patriotic obligation for the soldiers. Minnesotans believed that complete elimination of the Sioux was the only way to make the region safe and would finally bring the Sioux war to an end.

It was Brackett's aim to have the three companies attached to the Independent Battalion of Minnesota Cavalry, four companies, organized in the summer of 1863 under the command of Major Edwin A. C. Hatch. But General Pope had something else planned. Pope ordered the companies to organize as an independent battalion of their own. Brackett would be the obvious choice to command the unit. And so it came to be. The companies were organized as Brackett's Battalion of Minnesota Volunteer Cavalry with Major Alfred B. Brackett as commanding officer.

In order to be a full battalion, the unit needed a fourth company. One such company was already in place. The Second Minnesota Cavalry had mustered its companies the previous fall and in January was in training at Fort Snelling with thirteen companies — one company too many. The "thirteenth company," commanded by thirty-nine-year-old Ara Barton, was assigned to Brackett's Battalion. The battalion's first three companies, formerly companies G, I, and K, were redesignated as companies A, B, and C, respectively, with Barton's men as Company D. One of Barton's men, Private Stir S. Campbell, wrote in his diary, "got news that we belong to bratches batalion."

In 1858, Barton was appointed by Governor Sibley as lieutenant colonel of the Thirteenth Regiment of Minnesota Militia. After the

Dakota War, he enlisted as a private with the First Regiment of Minnesota Mounted Rangers in the fall of 1862. Later he was promoted to commissary sergeant and then first lieutenant of Company F. The regiment, which took part in battles against the Sioux in Dakota Territory in the summer of 1863, was mustered out of service after one year.

Captain Barton organized his new company mostly with new recruits. But several of the men came from his old company and other companies of the "First Mounted," including two sergeants and three corporals. Most of the men came from counties in the southeast corner of Minnesota. Forty-one of the recruits were from Olmsted County, twenty from the town of Marion alone. After the death of Corporal Zebina Lambert in March, Barton's company totaled one hundred men.

Among Barton's new recruits were a father and son. George Hoy, a millwright, and his son, Hugh, were from Bloomfield, Fillmore County. Originally from Canada, the Hoy family had settled in Fillmore County in 1858. Previously George had served in the LeColle Frontier Company of the Loyal Volunteers for the British army for seven years while residing in Odelltown, Quebec. During Quebec's rebellion of 1837–38 of French "patriots" against British "loyalists," George Hoy and his militia successfully defended the community of Odelltown from an attack by one thousand patriots in November 1838. The bloody battle of Odelltown resulted in more than one hundred patriot casualties with just a few British casualties, bringing an end to the rebellion. George was mustered out of the Loyal Volunteers in 1840 as a sergeant.

In 1862 George's wife passed away. In December of the following year, George decided to join Ara Barton's company, bringing his only child, Hugh, with him. George was forty-five years old, the age limit for volunteers, when he enlisted, but he declared himself to be forty-two years of age, probably just to make sure he would be accepted. Hugh was only fifteen, but at five feet, nine inches, he was tall for his age. Instead of claiming to be seventeen with parental consent, Hugh signed in as a nineteen-year-old. Hugh's physical stature may have fooled the recruiting officer in Bloomfield who was eager to accept the father-and-son package. The two were mustered in at Fort Snelling in January.

Brackett's Battalion settled into its quarters, a crudely constructed enclosure called the "pen" outside the walls of old Fort Snelling. At

Davenport, Iowa, the Fifth Iowa Cavalry gathered once again for its second term of service. The regiment replaced the vacated companies G, I, and K with new troops. After arriving in Nashville, the Fifth had a great deal of difficulty acquiring enough horses and arms, taking most of the spring to be re-equipped. Colonel Lowe was appointed as commander of the Third Cavalry Division, Army of the Cumberland. Lieutenant Colonel Patrick was assigned command of a brigade while Major Harlan Beard commanded the Fifth Iowa.

In June, the regiment returned to northern Alabama at Decatur. A month later, the Fifth Iowa and elements of four other regiments of veteran cavalry and a section of artillery were placed under the command of General Lovell H. Rousseau for a most daring expedition. The command marched deep into east-central Alabama, engaging in several skirmishes along the way, in a coordinated effort with General William T. Sherman's attack on Atlanta, Georgia. The raid succeeded in destroying millions of dollars of Confederate supplies, bridges, and railroads before reaching Opelika. Turning east, Rousseau's cavalry crossed the Chattahoochee River into Georgia where they continued to inflict damage on Confederate supply lines south of Atlanta.

The Fifth Iowa was then transferred to the command of General Edward M. McCook for another raid on the Confederate flank. McCook's raid was also successful in capturing and destroying a large quantity of Confederate supplies as well as taking several hundred prisoners. Then, while only a few miles south of Atlanta, McCook's luck changed. General Wheeler arrived with a large force of Confederate cavalry to the west, cutting off the Federals. McCook charged his command through the trap, crossed the Flint River, and raced for the Chattahoochee, fighting over every foot of ground along the way. Several hundred Federal cavalrymen were killed, wounded, or captured. Most of the wounded were left behind.

South of Franklin, McCook's battered and exhausted command began crossing the river by ferry when Wheeler's force arrived and immediately attacked. Most of the remaining Federals swam the river after abandoning their horses and weapons. Scattered across the countryside for several days, many of the men were killed or captured by Confederate citizens or guerrillas. The Fifth Iowa had lost several men during Rousseau's march into Alabama. During McCook's retreat, the regiment lost at least 120 men killed, wounded, and captured.

In early August, after the survivors of the Fifth Iowa were collected, no more than ninety men of the regiment could be mustered for duty. But Sherman's capture of Atlanta was critical and every man was needed for the effort. The small fragment of the Fifth took part in several more raids on Confederate supply lines close to Atlanta, suffering more losses in the process. During this time, the Fifth Iowa Infantry, which also had endured heavy losses and could no longer maintain regimental status, was consolidated with the Fifth Iowa Cavalry. The regiment was then renamed the Fifth Iowa Veteran Cavalry Consolidated. In October, with only thirty horses fit for service, the Fifth Iowa returned to Nashville to be remounted and re-equipped.

In November and December, the regiment was heavily involved in battles and skirmishes in central Tennessee as Confederate General John B. Hood, with his army, drove north in an attempt to capture Nashville. The Fifth also was engaged in the defense of the city as the southern army was defeated and driven back to Alabama. In March 1865 the Fifth Iowa again was involved in a major Union offensive thrust deep into the heart of Alabama, ultimately capturing Selma. As General Robert E. Lee surrendered his Confederate army to General Grant in Virginia, the Fifth Iowa arrived in Macon, Georgia. After the capture of Jefferson Davis, a detail of the Fifth assisted in the escorting and guarding of the former Confederate president.

Returning to Nashville in August, the Fifth Iowa Cavalry was mustered out of service on the eleventh after serving a long and distinguished career over a large part of the South. Colonel William W. Lowe received several commendations for gallant and meritorious service in several battles and skirmishes. He was mustered out of volunteer service in January 1865, returning to the regular U.S. Army. At Fort Leavenworth, Kansas, Lowe served as acting assistant provost marshal general, superintendent of volunteer recruiting, and chief mustering and disbursing officer for Kansas, Nebraska, Dakota, and Colorado. He was brevetted colonel and brigadier general for his services in the war and was promoted to major in the Sixth U.S. Cavalry. He left the army in 1869 after sixteen years of service.

As for Brackett's Battalion, a new experience in the cavalry was about to begin in the spring of 1864. The three veteran companies were brought back to full strength by taking on new recruits to replace their losses in the South.

Company A was led by Captain Henning von Minden, First Lieutenant August Matthaus, and Second Lieutenant Joseph Buck. The leadership of Company B remained unsettled following Captain Smith's resignation in January. His replacement was left in question until June when Lieutenant John A. Reed was appointed captain. Marshall Fall and George S. Converse, both originally corporals in the company, were then appointed as the company's lieutenants. Robert H. Rose, originally the company's first sergeant and later first lieutenant, was promoted to major and transferred to the Second Minnesota Cavalry.

Company C still maintained its original officers with Captain Erwin Shelley, First Lieutenant Mortimer Neely, and Second Lieutenant Robert W. Peckham. In Company D, Captain Barton's officers were First Lieutenant George G. Wilder, once a sergeant with the First Minnesota Mounted Rangers, and Second Lieutenant Joseph H. Porter.

Eugene Marshall had begun his service with the third company as a private. During his two years in the South, Marshall had risen to sergeant after holding every grade of corporal and sergeant in between. He had caught the attention of Major Brackett who viewed Marshall as a steady, level-headed soldier who had gained a great deal of respect from the men. As the battalion was being organized, Brackett believed Marshall would be the man to hold one of the most important positions in the unit and so promoted him to battalion sergeant major.

As spring approached and the battalion's new recruits drilled at the fort, the men soon learned of their new mission. They would be marching to Dakota Territory in pursuit of hostile Indians. The new assignment was deeply rooted in the whites' long mistrust of Indians. But in a larger sense, it was a result of an unjust and serious mishandling of the Indians.

Prior to the start of the Civil War, the Sioux or Dakota in Minnesota were granted reservation land along the Minnesota River and promised annuity payments of cash and goods in exchange for lands to be settled by the growing white population. But the agreement was filled with holes as the Sioux were cheated out of their money by local traders and unscrupulous government officials. To add to the indignities, the Sioux again made agreements with the government to secure more cash by surrendering more of the reservation land along the river. But again the payments were slow in coming or scooped up by other interests. Added to that, a crop failure on the reservation in 1861 brought the tribes to near starvation.

While annuity payments were still delayed and the government failed to supply the Sioux with food, the Indians' response to the white man had swelled to explosive proportions. In August 1862, the Sioux lashed out, attacking farmsteads and settlements in western Minnesota. Many whites—men, women, and children—were brutally murdered on the prairies, causing panic across the state. Refugees fled to larger towns and military outposts, depopulating the area as an all-out war began.

Militia units sprang up throughout the state, and more volunteer regiments were quickly mustered. Several battles took place across the frontier before the Sioux were decisively defeated in September at the Battle of Wood Lake in Yellow Medicine County. It was estimated that approximately five hundred civilians were killed during the outbreak as well as about one hundred soldiers.

In the aftermath, thirty-eight of the Dakota, convicted of committing murder or rape, were executed in a mass hanging at Mankato on December 26. Later, the remaining Dakota, including peaceful bands who took no part in the conflict, were rounded up, banished from the state, and relocated on reservations in Dakota Territory and Nebraska.

Most of the warring Dakota who avoided capture during the conflict fled west into Dakota Territory where, it was believed, they joined other Sioux tribes in an attempt to threaten further white expansion and possibly recross the border to make more attacks. Minnesotans still shuddered from fear of the Indian menace and demanded protection of their western border.

The Federal government agreed. But the government's interests were much broader. With the discovery of gold in Idaho Territory and the government's encouragement of western settlement, troops would be needed to deal with the hostile Sioux. The military would also assist in making land treaties with the peaceful tribes and establish military outposts across the region to protect the miners, traders, and settlers traveling across the northern plains.

General Henry H. Sibley was given command of the Military District of Minnesota. Sibley, the state's first governor, commanded the army against the Sioux during the war. He preferred to return to civilian life and politics after the conflict but was urged by General Pope to accept the new position as an award for his handling of the campaign.

General Alfred Sully, an experienced Indian fighter, was placed in command of the Military District of Iowa. A graduate of West Point, Sully was once the colonel of the First Minnesota Infantry with the Army of the Potomac and later a brigade commander. Greatly agitated by the new post assignment, he preferred to remain in the East to fight in the war against the Confederate rebellion but reluctantly accepted his new assignment in the West. Sully was well suited for the assignment. Before the Civil War, he had spent part of his military service in Minnesota where he gained experience in Indian fighting and developed a keen sense of Indian behavior.

In the spring of 1863, Pope designed a two-pronged expedition for his two commanders who would march into Dakota Territory against the Sioux. Sibley would march his brigade, comprised of three regiments of Minnesota infantry, the First Minnesota Mounted Rangers, and the Third Minnesota Battery of Light Artillery, northwest out of Minnesota into Dakota Territory. Sully and his brigade, consisting of cavalrymen of the Sixth and Seventh Iowa, the Second Nebraska, and a battery of howitzers, would ascend the Missouri River from Sioux City, Iowa, cut off the Sioux escape from Sibley's westward drive, and eventually link up with the Minnesota brigade.

The campaign proved to be something less than a success. After entering Dakota Territory, Sibley discovered that the report of a massive buildup of hostile Sioux was false and that no such party was to be found. Then in July, because of a young, nervous warrior who murdered one of Sibley's surgeons, the Minnesota brigade attacked camps of Sioux, of whom few played any part in the Minnesota war, in three fierce battles at Big Mound, Dead Buffalo Lake, and Stony Lake. Some of the people fled north into British Canada, never to return. Others were chased across the Missouri River where Sibley called off the pursuit. After several days of searching for Sully's column without success, Sibley returned to Minnesota.

Due to a severe drought in the region and low water on the Missouri, Sully's brigade was slow in its march north. He finally reached the appointed meeting place a month after Sibley had left. But Sully still managed to make his expedition worthwhile. The Sioux who fought Sibley returned to the east side of the river to reclaim their hunting grounds, believing the threat had passed. Sully found a massive camp of several thousand Indians at the base of Whitestone Hill. A portion of the brigade arrived at the camp ahead of the main force and began to talk with the leaders. But just as Sibley's encounter had ended in violence, so did this one.

The rest of the brigade finally arrived and saw only that their advance party was surrounded by Indians. Sully's troops immediately attacked the camp, slashing and shooting at every Indian in sight. Men, women, and children were scattered in every direction. The Sioux warriors fought back bravely until darkness ended the battle, allowing the Indians to escape across the prairie.

To Sully and Sibley, the expedition was a success. More than three hundred Indians were killed in the battles and about 150 prisoners were rounded up by Sully's troops, mostly terrified women and children. Nearly all of the tribes' winter food supplies and equipment were destroyed. But in reality, the attacks made by Sully and Sibley were a cruel injustice to the Sioux who played no part in the war. The Indians of the northern plains were enraged and now presented an even greater threat to white expansion in the West.

In 1864, Pope ordered a second expedition into Dakota Territory, nearly identical to the previous year's campaign. Named the Northwestern Indian Expedition, the campaign was to be conducted by two brigades of cavalry with a battery of artillery in each. The First Brigade would assemble at Sioux City, Iowa, under the direct command of General Sully. This brigade would consist of the Sixth Regiment of Iowa Cavalry, three companies of the Seventh Iowa Cavalry, all of the two companies of the First Dakota Cavalry, Brackett's Battalion, and Pope's Battery of four twelve-pound mountain howitzers commanded by Captain Nathaniel Pope.

The Second Brigade again was an all-Minnesota brigade formed by the mounted regiment of the Eighth Minnesota Infantry, six companies of the Second Minnesota Cavalry, and the Third Minnesota Battery of Light Artillery under Captain John Jones consisting of two six-pound smooth bore guns and two twelve-pound mountain howitzers. Assembling at Fort Ridgely, Minnesota, the Second Brigade, commanded by Colonel Minor T. Thomas of the Eighth Minnesota, would march west to the Missouri River where it would join the First Brigade marching from Sioux City. General Sully was to be the expedition's overall commander.

In the spring, Brackett's Battalion was armed with Sharps carbines,

Colt Navy revolvers, and the new model light cavalry sabers, a great improvement over the arms they were issued in 1862. All the men were armed with sabers, and nearly all of them had both carbine and pistol. Satisfied with their firepower, their concern now was over their mounts.

The army had purchased horses from Canada for the expedition's Minnesota troops. The "Canadian ponies," a smaller breed of horse, were brought to a depot in Detroit, Michigan. From there they were shipped by train to La Crosse, Wisconsin. In April a detail of Brackett's Battalion went to La Crosse to receive the horses. At Fort Snelling the men were in disbelief at what they saw when the horses arrived on the twenty-second.

The animals were in poor condition due to the lack of proper care in Detroit and the long, tiring train ride to La Crosse. But the men were mostly concerned by the horses' size. They failed to understand how these undersized horses, smaller than the mounts they used in the South, could endure the weight of a cavalryman and his equipment and stand up to several hundred miles of marching over the open plains in the summer heat.

During their two years in the South, the veterans learned to travel light on their marches for the sake of the horses. Now the men realized they would have to find ways to travel even lighter yet if the ponies were going to survive. Brackett was ordered to march the battalion out of Fort Snelling for Sioux City on May 2. This gave the men only eleven days to get the ponies in shape. Many of the new recruits had little or no experience with horses, and most of the horses had little or no experience with riders.

# Sully's Troops March

ON MAY 2, Brackett's Battalion marched out of Fort Snelling with its company and battalion wagons each drawn by teams of six mules. There was also an additional train of twenty-six wagons loaded with supplies for the First Brigade, drawn by fifty yokes of oxen. It took a few days for the men to get accustomed to their new horses. By the morning of the second day when the column began its march, one of the old veterans was still experiencing problems with his horse. One of the tallest and longest-legged troopers in the battalion, he had gained a notorious reputation for being severe on horse flesh. Described as exhibiting the correct number of "sheets in the wind" with "Texan ornaments jingling at the heels," the man still had not sobered from the previous night's drinking

As the column moved out, this man's horse stood still. Spurring his pony harder with every kick only produced loud laughs from the rest of the troops as they marched by. Still the horse refused to move. Someone finally pointed out to the man that his spurs actually were not touching the horse at all. He then learned he had been spurring his own legs under the lean pony, shredding the bottom of his pants legs. One man yelled out as he passed by, "Put the spurs on the calf of your leg and you'll fetch 'im."

After crossing the Minnesota River at Belle Plaine and again at St. Peter, the battalion entered Blue Earth County passing by Mankato, heading southwest. On the ninth, it entered the town of Garden City, Minnesota, where it would camp on the Wantonwan River. The townspeople were expecting the arrival of Brackett's Battalion. When the column entered the town, a committee approached Major Brackett with a request on behalf of Company B.

The company was still referred to as the "Blue Earth County Cavalry." Even though most of company's fifty-six new recruits were not from the county, the townspeople and neighboring farmers turned out to welcome them with wagonloads of food. Eleven men from Garden City had previously served or were currently serving in the company. Brackett ordered Company B to fall out as the rest of the battalion headed for camp at the river.

In a letter to the *Mankato Weekly Record,* Lieutenant Reed described the reception his company received:

> Then a concentrated movement was made, and all those good things were piled upon a table, and this table did fairly groan under the load. And then Company "B" was called upon and ordered to charge upon these good things aforesaid. This they did in right gallant style, taking into consideration the fact that it would probably be many a long day before another opportunity would occur for action like this. But Company "B" for once failed—failed to clear the table—but they did all that men could do—the task was too great; and they retired in good order. In the evening all repaired to the Farmer's Hall, and participated in a grand dance. The ladies of Garden City evidently did not consider it beneath their dignity to dance with a soldier, perchance his clothes were dusty from his long day's ride. No, not they, they strove to interest and comfort those that were about to leave civilization upon their long and dreary march, and they succeeded most admirably. For all of these courtesies we feel thankful, but not until we shall be far away from friends, and hard tack and bacon become our fare for a long time, can we fully appreciate it. Bully for Garden City! You have every vote in Company "B" for county seat.[1]

Continuing their march, the battalion passed through Jackson before entering Iowa and passing by Spirit Lake. On the nineteenth, twenty-one-year-old William T. Plummer of Company C died from disease. He had been with the company for only fifty days. On the twenty-first, Brackett's Battalion reached Sioux City, making camp on the bank of the Missouri. From Fort Snelling they had marched 325 miles. The men learned that the long march had little effect on the health of the small Canadian ponies. The horses reached Sioux City with a surprising amount of endurance and proved their gait at a walk was no less than larger mounts. In a letter to the *Saint Paul Weekly Press,* George Northrup wrote, "The 'Press' spoke disparagingly of our horses on their first arrival at the fort. They are small, it is true, probably too small to mount our cavalry at the South, but for this expedition, are superior to those elephantine quadrupeds which are suddenly reduced to skin and bones, by traveling out 'sight of the forage train."[2] The army had learned something about horses from the Plains Indians by acquiring the same kind of mounts to fight them.

Before they arrived at Sioux City, the troops were unsure of what this season's campaign would produce. Some were eager for a battle with the Indians, hoping to reap revenge for their home state. Others were satisfied that Sibley's and Sully's expeditions of the previous year had beaten the Sioux into submission, and they were no longer a threat. In a letter to his sister in March, Eugene Marshall expressed his thoughts: "These Indian wars are a great humbug. I expect that for the next few months after [the] grass starts we shall go on some wild goose chase across the plains toward the Missouri River. I expect that the expedition will be more of the nature of a pleasure trip than anything else."[3] After arriving at Sioux City, the men obtained new information that cleared up any doubts they had about what lay ahead.

At his headquarters in Sioux City, General Sully began to realize that the campaign of 1863 had not been as successful as it was first believed. For several weeks before the First Brigade collected at Sioux City, scouts had been sent out into Dakota Territory to determine the condition and attitude of the various Sioux tribes. Rather than taking a peaceful stance in the region, Sully learned that the tribes were beginning to band together to resist the expedition and were expecting to give Sully a battle in defense of their lands. Sully had hoped to make treaties with the Sioux and resolve hostilities peacefully. But with the new information, Sully announced to the troops, "With our columns united we will move to a point where, I am informed, the Indians await me in large numbers to give me battle."

After preparing their supplies and equipment, the various units of the First Brigade marched out of Sioux City on different days to rendezvous at Fort Sully. Situated on the east side of the Missouri, about fifteen miles below the abandoned Fort Pierre, the post was originally named Fort Bartlett. Sully's troops had reestablished the post after the previous year's campaign, renaming it Fort Sully. Brackett's Battalion left Sioux City on May 31, marching well over two hundred miles before reaching the fort on June 15.

Small bands of Indians were already making their presence known as they launched attempts to disrupt the progress of Sully's brigade.

At a camp about eighty miles above Sioux City, the horses of a detachment of the Seventh Iowa were stampeded by Indians. In another incident, after Brackett's Battalion arrived at the fort, Barton's company crossed the river and marched southwest in an attempt to recover horses stampeded out of Fort Randall farther down the Missouri. Returning unsuccessful, Company D marched 130 miles in three days.

On June 26, the First Brigade marched north from Fort Sully destined for a rendezvous point with the Second Brigade farther upriver. On the twenty-eighth as Sully continued his march, Captain John Fielner, the expedition's topographical engineer, wandered from the column. A favorite of Sully, Fielner was prone to straying from the rest of the troops to study the landscape without heeding the existing dangers. On this day he stopped to examine a large rock opposite the mouth of the Cheyenne River. Three Indians lying in ambush shot and killed the captain.

After Fielner's body was discovered, a company of Dakota Cavalry spotted the three Indians and gave chase. After a long pursuit over hills and through ravines, the cavalrymen finally caught up with the attackers, killing all three. The heads of the Indians were removed and brought into Sully's camp that night. The next morning Sully ordered a detail to place the Indian heads on poles that were erected on a high hill as a warning to any hostiles in the area. News of Sully's action spread quickly across the plains and through the Sioux camps as far north as Canada, further stiffening the Sioux determination to resist the invaders.

George Northrup took the event casually. In a letter to his brother-in-law, Henry Cole in LaFayette, New York, Northrup wrote, "I enclose a lock of hair from one of the heads, it is yet bloody, but if you wish to preserve it you can wash it out."

On the thirtieth, the First Brigade made camp near the mouth of Swan Lake Creek. The next day Colonel Thomas's Second Brigade reached the camp, having marched more than three hundred miles from Fort Ridgely. Sully was not pleased by what Thomas's command had brought in tow, an emigrant wagon train of about 150 wagons drawn by slow moving oxen with an estimated 250 people and a herd of cattle.

After leaving Fort Ridgely, the Second Brigade stopped at Wood Lake, Minnesota, in Yellow Medicine County where the wagon train was waiting for their arrival. Led by Thomas Holmes, the emigrants consisted mostly of miners with a large number of women and children, all destined for the Idaho goldfields, which lay in the newly created Montana Territory. Holmes had been promised by General Sibley that a military escort across the now dangerous Dakota Territory would be provided. When the Second Brigade reached Wood Lake, Colonel Thomas knew he was compelled to bring the Holmes expedition with him.

The next day the Northwestern Indian Expedition, with Holmes's wagon train, took up its line of march north along the Missouri, heading for a site on the river prearranged by Sully for the location of another new fort. Sully wanted to avoid marching both brigades in a single column. A line of march in that manner would stretch for several miles, leaving various segments vulnerable to attack. Due to the flatness of the terrain, however, Sully found it possible to march the expedition in a wide, close-grouped formation.

The First Brigade marched with its supply wagons in two columns, 150 yards apart. The general and his staff rode in the center followed by the provost guard, scouts, Pope's Battery, and the ambulance wagons. The Seventh Iowa, Brackett's Battalion, and the Dakota Cavalry rode in a column on the left flank, sixty paces from the left wagon column. The Sixth Iowa rode in a column sixty paces outside of the right wagon column. The advance guard consisted of one company of cavalry with scouts, one and a half miles ahead of the command. One company of cavalry followed closely behind the command as the rear guard. Loose stock, horses, and cattle were contained between the columns of wagons. The Second Brigade followed in the same style formation with the settlers' wagon train in the center. In this manner the expedition marched in a column about 275 yards wide.

The drought that hampered Sully's march in 1863 had continued into 1864. With temperatures reaching 106 degrees in the shade, the Dakota prairie was parched. What little grass that would have been left for the animals of the expedition was grazed away by the massive herds of buffalo who had long since moved on in search of better forage. However, enough vegetation was found along streams and small rivers to sustain the animals.

Firewood was scarce as well, in fact, most of the time it was nonexistent. But dried buffalo dung, called buffalo chips, was plentiful and a proven efficient fuel. The troops found they could easily collect the chips in a short period of time for their fires.

On July 8, the expedition reached a point on the Missouri opposite the mouth of the Cannonball River. No buffalo had been seen during the march over the open prairie, although evidence of their presence was abundant. But here, at the mouth of the Cannonball, the soldiers and emigrants found themselves surrounded by buffalo numbering in the thousands.

Three steamboats loaded with supplies had come up the river to meet the expedition. Sully crossed the river to locate a spot, established earlier, where the new fort would be built. A short distance north of the Cannonball, Sully's troops, wagons, and the Holmes wagon train crossed the river on the steamers. At the landing on the west side, a sign greeted everyone. The inscription on the board read, "Fort Rice: Located by Brig. Gen. Sully, July 7th, 1864." The new post was named after General Clay Rice who, while with the Army of the Potomac, had been killed in battle only two months earlier.

It took two days for the crossing to be made, the last troops making the trip on the tenth. Along with fort provisions and supplies for the expedition, the steamers unloaded tons of building material for the fort. Five companies of the Thirtieth Wisconsin Infantry also came up on the steamers to construct and garrison Fort Rice. The fort would be built on suitable tableland several feet above the river with groves of cottonwood nearby. Fort Rice was to be Sully's base of operations.

# Battle of Killdeer Mountain

SULLY'S PLAN was for the expedition to march as far as the Yellowstone River near the mouth of the Powder River, deep into eastern Montana Territory, where he intended to establish another military post. Military authorities in Minnesota promised that the Holmes wagon train would have an escort as far as the Yellowstone. From there it was believed the emigrants could travel to the Idaho goldfields safely on their own. For more than a week, the troops made preparations for the march while the horses, mules, and oxen rested. The soldiers were now fully expecting a fight with the Indians. The miners also used the time to rest their animals and make repairs on their wagons.

The region between the Missouri and the Yellowstone was virtually unknown to white men. No formal maps of the area existed. The only guides Sully had available to him were crude maps and descriptions made by miners, trappers, and hunters who had ventured into the area before hostilities with the Indians began. Sully had about one hundred Indian and mixed-blood scouts with him, but even they had no knowledge of the region. Captain von Minden was now the expedition's topographical engineer. It would be up to him to make an accurate record of the area over which they would travel.

During this time, Sully's scouts came into camp with a report about the Sioux location. The hostile tribes had been seen in a large camp near the headwaters of the Cannonball River. The number of warriors was estimated to be about six thousand. Not at that time or any time in the future would Sully realize the actual number of warriors he was going to engage was little more than one-fourth that number. On July 17, Sully and his staff visited the Idaho emigrants to inform them of his intentions. "Gentlemen, I am damn sorry you are here," Sully announced, "but so long as you are, I will do the best I can to protect you. . . . I expect to jump an Indian camp and give them hell." After a few reassuring words, the miners responded with cheers.

Early in the morning of the nineteenth, the Northwestern Indian Expedition began its march from Fort Rice, heading southwest for the Cannonball River. The massive formation included supply wagons drawn by a hundred teams of mules and more than forty ox-drawn wagons followed by the Holmes wagon train. Nearing the Cannonball, the wide formation had to be changed to a narrower column due to the increasingly rough terrain. Stretching for more than three miles, the column was now more vulnerable to Indian attack. Upon reaching the river, the water was found to be clear and sweet, the best water the troops had had since leaving Sioux City or, for the Second Brigade, since leaving Minnesota.

No Indians had been observed as the expedition marched west along the river, although evidence of their presence was becoming more apparent. During the day, smoke from the Indians' fires could be discerned on distant hilltops, and at night, flaming arrows were seen arching in the sky. The Sioux were closely watching the movements of the troops, signaling each other about the army's progress.

After marching about a hundred miles along the Cannonball, Sully discovered the abandoned site of an Indian village. Discouraged for a short time, Sully now believed his scouts were intentionally misleading him away from the main body of Sioux. Using his own instincts and reports from other scouts, Sully turned his march northwest. He now believed that the village he was looking for rested approximately eighty miles north near the headwaters of the Knife River.

Rising from the valley of the Cannonball, the land leveled out, making the march less difficult. But the summer's drought was still taking a toll on the expedition. Swarms of locusts had devoured what little vegetation was left on the flatlands except for large areas of cactus. Frequently the temperature rose to more than one hundred degrees in the shade. The giant cloud of dust worked up by the animals and wagons filled everyone's eyes and nostrils, aggravating their thirst. What little water could be found was alkaline, making it unfit for animals and humans. Often the animals could not be restrained from drinking the bad water, which left them in yet poorer health. At one campsite, some of the mules and horses broke loose from their picket lines and stampeded into a mud hole for relief. On the trail, many of the cattle, oxen, mules, and cavalry horses gave out and had to be shot.

On the twenty-fourth, several miles south of the Knife River, the expedition reached the Heart River. There the scouts came in and gave details of sighting the Indian camp. Located about a two days' march to the north, the village reportedly contained sixteen hundred lodges, which later proved to be an accurate count. But the overestimation of six thousand warriors was still accepted as true.

Sully made camp on the river where the expedition would rest for a day and make preparations for battle. The emigrant train was corralled with the military supply wagons. A detail from the Second Minnesota Cavalry along with other cavalrymen who lost their mounts on the trail would remain for protection. Sully planned to begin his march early in the morning of the twenty-sixth before sunrise. Light marching orders were given. The men were ordered to leave their shelter tents behind and take nothing with them except a small amount of rations, their weapons, and ammunition. In his diary Marshall recorded a portion of the marching orders: "Rec'd orders to corral the wagons & get ready to march tomorrow with two days' cooked rations in haversacks and five days' on pack mules. One hundred rounds of carbine ammunition and twenty-four rounds of pistol ammunition to each man."[1] Extra ammunition would be carried by the pack mules.

Late into the night as the troops prepared, a problem developed with the pack-mule equipment; no pack saddle blankets could be found. But enough gunny sacks were gathered to solve the problem when another problem arose. The soft, cotton webbed bands that, when cinched under the bellies of the mules, secured the packs were also missing. Instead, the men substituted narrow, hard leather straps, which drove the mules wild with discomfort. Sully was forced to abandon the pack-mule system in exchange for light wagons. As a result, the troops were late in beginning their march. The first groups started out at noon on the twenty-sixth, with the last leaving camp at 3:00 P.M.

Early into the march, a few of the scouts rode back from the front reporting that the advance company, several miles ahead, was involved in a fierce fight near a place called "Young Man Butte." Sully turned to Major Brackett and ordered him to take his battalion forward into the skirmish. On the way, the battalion met several men of the advance company, most of them drunk, returning from the fight, reporting that the rest of the company was surrounded. It took Brackett's Battalion three hours to reach the tall butte where the skirmish took place, finding that the cavalrymen had retreated unharmed and the small party of Indians gone.

Men in the other units were not the only ones finding it convenient to indulge in alcohol. In Brackett's Battalion, Captain Shelley and Lieutenant Neely, among others, were still up to their old tricks. As the four companies raced for the butte, Brackett had to deal with the two men along the way. Marshall wrote,

> He went off to the right where Comp. C was and commenced urging them on in advance of the centre. Lieut. Neely was in command of the Comp., & he too was very drunk and behaved disgracefully. Maj. B_____ got excited & chased the Capt. a while with his sabre. Comp. C were almost in condition to mutiny on account of the conduct of Lieut. N.[2]

The battalion marched two or three miles past the butte, then stopped to wait for the rest of the command. There the two brigades made camp for the night. Sully knew they were close to the Sioux village. To conceal their presence as much as possible, no campfires were allowed for the night. The soldiers slept on the ground with their arms while many of the horses were kept saddled. Before sunrise on the twenty-seventh, the march resumed in what turned out to be an uneventful day.

In the first hour of July 28 the men began to break camp. Sully knew he would meet the Sioux on this day. One clue was the absence of several of his scouts. He later learned they had deserted the expedition to join the Sioux. Thus the Indians would be aware of when the soldiers would begin their march. The cavalrymen saddled their mounts and made preparations as quietly as they could. Then one shot broke the silence. "While saddling his horse," Marshall wrote, "Major B_____'s pistol was accidentally discharged in the holster, & he was wounded in two places in the hand but not very severely."

The command marched out of camp at 3:00 A.M. led by the First Brigade. At about 10:00 A.M., after marching several miles over dry rolling prairie, the forward scouts returned with news of the location of the Sioux camp, about ten miles ahead. Sully brought the troops into battle formation with the Second Brigade on the left of the First. Six companies of the Sixth Iowa Cavalry along with the three companies of the Seventh Iowa were dismounted and brought to the front as skirmishers. To their left were six companies of the Eighth Minnesota, also dismounted. Pope's Battery was placed in the center of the skirmish line supported by the Dakota Cavalry with the Third Minnesota Battery and four companies of cavalry in reserve. Brackett's Battalion remained mounted in a column of squadrons on the right flank as was the Second Minnesota Cavalry on the left flank. The supply and ambulance wagons closed up in the center to the rear as three more companies followed the formation as the rear guard.

With the skirmishers spread apart by a few paces between each man, the formation began its march forward in the form of a large hollow square nearly a mile in width. Shortly, the Sioux warriors made their appearance in small groups on hills to the right and left of the soldiers, some mounted on ponies, others on foot. Many years later, Eugene Marshall described the scene for the *St. Paul Weekly Press.*

> As our column approached they advanced, covering the prairie for miles in every direction, and occupying with small squads every hill top and vantage ground in sight. There was no mass of warriors either in line or column, to give the idea of resistance and power, but scattered bands, moving in every direction . . . all dressed in their gayest paints, leggins and headdresses, as if for a day of pleasure instead of a desperate battle. Confident of success, they swarmed in ever increasing numbers, which in comparison dwarfed our little command to a mere handful. Stationed on every hill top, warriors signaled each other by flashes of sunlight from the small mirrors which all seemed to carry, while others, with long batons fringed with horse hair and decorated with eagle feathers, waved them backward and forward to direct the movements of those in the valleys. Their code of signals seemed to be perfectly understood by every warrior. As our little column advanced, numbers who had not been seen before occupied the hill tops in our rear, and, completely surrounding us, yelled in derision at our seeming insignificance.[3]

Marching farther, Sully's troops came within view of the village. A mass of sixteen hundred white, cone-shaped lodges of dressed buffalo skins filled the horizon five miles ahead. The village was located at the foot of a range of high buttes known to the Indians as "the place where they kill the deer," or to the white man, Killdeer Mountain. The mountain was broken into sharp, abrupt heights, with deep, narrow gorges filled with thickets of brushwood and timber. The location gave the appearance of a paradise with beautiful springs gushing from the hillsides. In front of the village stretched a broad expanse of prairie, broken by deep ravines that provided excellent cover for the warriors.

Among the many Sioux tribes that made up the small city were the Hunkpapa, Oglala, Yanktonai, and many other bands of Teton. The Hunkpapa originally occupied the site before other tribes swelled the camp, knowing that Sully's expedition was marching from Sioux City and Fort Ridgely. Most of the bands were hoping to avoid an encounter with the soldiers but now realized they were compelled to defend themselves. A vast majority of these Indians had not played any part in the Minnesota conflict.

Inkpaduta, the notorious leader who led a renegade band of Dakota in the massacres of white settlers in Iowa and Minnesota in 1857, had distanced himself from the Minnesota war, remaining in self-exile in Dakota Territory. Avoided by peaceful tribes since that time, the outlaw chief brought his band of Dakota and Yanktonai into the Killdeer Mountain camp to lend them his skills as an experienced warrior against the white man. The other tribes, realizing there was strength in numbers, accepted his presence.

At the village was the leader of the Hunkpapa, Sitting Bull. At the age of thirty-three, in the early years of his rise to power among the Sioux, Sitting Bull also hoped that he and his people could avoid a confrontation with the military. One year earlier, when Sibley's brigade fought the Sioux east of the Missouri, Sitting Bull's only contact with the soldiers had taken place when he and a few other warriors chased Sibley's supply wagons in a running skirmish that resulted in capturing only one mule. Now for the first time, the Hunkpapa leader was about to confront white soldiers in a head-to-head battle.

With his nephew, White Bull, Sitting Bull joined others at the top of a nearby hill to observe the soldiers moving over the prairie. In later years Sitting Bull described the scene:

> We could see a whole army of soldiers coming from the southeast. Their line of foot soldiers was a mile wide, horsemen followed, and behind them was a string of wagons.
>
> In our group was a Sioux named Long Dog. His medicine was strong that day, he was bullet proof, so he volunteered to approach

the soldiers and ride along their front to see if they would shoot at him. As he raced down the line, many soldiers shot at him, but he was not hit. The whites had started the war, so the Sioux shot back. When Long Dog decided to show off his power a second time, White Bull decided to show his bravery also and rode down the front of the soldiers' lines with him. Neither man was hit. I was glad my nephew had taken this opportunity to show such courage in his first battle.[4]

The taunting by the two warriors prompted the soldiers to fire the first shots, beginning the battle. The Indians were confident they would be victorious, so much so that when the battle commenced no preparations were made to evacuate families. Women, children, and the elderly crowded in front of the village to witness the defeat of the soldiers. Some of the warriors carried firearms, consisting mainly of old rifles, muskets, and even flintlocks. Most of them carried only bows, lances, and war clubs. The soldiers were surprised by the horsemanship skills the Indians displayed as the warriors shot their arrows from the backs of their ponies at a full gallop. But most of these Sioux had never before experienced the firepower of carbines and artillery.

The fighting became general, but the soldiers kept their line of march in good order as they pressed on toward the village. Small groups of warriors attacked Sully's troops from all sides as the soldiers adjusted their formation to repel the threats with a hail of carbine fire. The only thing that made the soldiers hesitate were the "unearthly screams" the warriors made in their attacks. The Sioux attempted to attack the rear of the command and capture the supply wagons, but the rear guard easily drove them off. At one point a portion of the Second Minnesota Cavalry dismounted to shore up the left flank of the Eighth Minnesota. Later, the Second dismounted more companies, sweeping to the left to fend off a threatening formation of Sioux.

The artillery was occupied making well-directed shots at Indian formations in deep ravines and on distant hills. The loud blasts from the cannons and the exploding shells in the midst of Indian concentrations shocked the Sioux. They had no conception of the range and destructive power of the batteries. Sitting Bull recalled, "I had never seen white troops fight before. The number of guns and the amount of shooting was much more than I had ever expected, and the cannon which shot so loud and so far and so often was a big surprise."[5]

The Sioux took every opportunity to remove their fallen comrades from the field. Pairs of mounted Indians were sometimes seen sweeping a dead or wounded man off the ground at a full gallop in front of deadly fire. One mounted Sioux, in a hail of bullets, was observed throwing a lariat around the neck of a dead warrior, successfully dragging the body off the battleground at full speed. Sitting Bull recalled the differences in behavior of the opposing forces during his first battle against government troops:

> I concluded the white soldiers did not know how to fight. They are not lively enough. They stand still and run straight; it is easy to shoot them. They do not try to save themselves. Also, they seem to have no hearts. When an Indian is killed, the other Indians feel sorry and cry, and sometimes stop fighting. But when a white soldier gets killed, nobody cries, nobody cares; they go right on shooting and let him lie there. Sometimes they even go off and leave their wounded behind them.[6]

Sitting Bull also described how his people would take the opportunity to die a glorious death as a warrior:

> That day there was a special act of courage I shall never forget. We had in our tribe a man known as The Man Who Never Walked. He had been born a cripple, his arms and limbs were badly deformed so he could not walk or go on the warpath as the other young men. He chose this occasion as a good day to die. As the soldiers came close to our camp, he asked a friend to place him in a basket on a travois and head the horse straight toward the enemy so he could meet his maker as a warrior. The horse galloped straight toward the soldiers, until a bullet cut him down, throwing The Man Who Never Walked from the travois. There he sat facing the oncoming soldiers, singing his death song until the soldiers bullets put an end to his life. Because of his great courage, we always referred to him thereafter as Bear's Heart.[7]

On the right side of the soldiers' skirmish line, Major Brackett brought up two companies of his battalion for support, pressing forward in that manner for about three miles. A lone Indian on foot, in the distance to the right of Brackett's Battalion, was spotted by Corporal James Edwards of Company B. Edwards's father had been killed by the Sioux near his home near Butternut, west of Mankato, during the 1862 war. The twenty-three-year-old corporal, born in Wales, was informed of his father's death in a letter while serving in Tennessee with the Fifth Iowa. James vowed he would some day have revenge.

Now, while acting as one of the orderlies for the major, Edwards saw his opportunity. Drawing his saber, he started at a full gallop in pursuit of the Indian, shouting at the top of his voice, "Now is the time for revenge." A group of Indians realized the dilemma of their comrade and detailed a small party to assist him. Perceiving this, Captain Reed dispatched an equal number of his men to the aid of Edwards. For a moment, the battle on that part of the field stopped as both Indians and soldiers watched the two parties race toward each other at a right angle, converging on one spot. The corporal, focused only on one thing, soon overran the warrior. Many years later, Isaac Botsford recalled the incident:

> When Jim had almost overtaken him, the Indian suddenly turned, and waiting until the last moment, with his gun pointed directly at Jim's head, he took deliberate aim and fired. Jim was young, active and strong in those days. With one jerk on his bridle, he threw his horse back on his haunches, which elevated his head just enough to receive the fatal bullet designed for Jim's brain. The horse dropped dead.[8]

With both men now on the ground, the Indian swung his empty gun by the barrel at his attacker. Edwards parried the blow with his saber and with his first thrust killed the warrior. The Sioux rescue party stopped and turned back. Edwards collected the Indian's gun and moccasins, pulled the bridle and saddle from his dead horse, and returned to the battalion. Botsford wrote, "Jim was the hero of the hour; his revenge was complete."

Later, a large force of Sioux began massing on Brackett's right. Company B was dismounted to skirmish with them while Brackett sent a message to the general informing him of the situation, requesting permission to make a charge against the Indian party. Permission was granted. Brackett turned to the one company most experienced in leading a charge, his old company, the one he had recruited, Company C. Despite the reputation of its officers, the company was again called on to do what it had done so many times in the South with the Fifth Iowa.

With sabers drawn, Captain Shelley led the company in a charge that was executed in a wide sweeping turn, starting from the right and gradually turning to the left. The charge drove the Indians for two or three miles toward the hills. The rest of the battalion followed closely for support. Sergeant Major Eugene Marshall now found himself in a bad situation:

> I became separated from the command and was surrounded by four Indians, two mounted & two dismounted; & before I got away had a lively time receiving two arrow[s], wound[ing] me in the left hip and one in the left side. They were shot at about twenty feet distance, but though the surgeon thinks one of them pretty severe, I am not very badly hurt. The speed & endurance of my horse which ran away with me in the first instance—and a chance shot from a straggler who had fallen behind the company [were the reasons] that I got off.[9]

A few days later, Marshall wrote a letter to the *St. Paul Weekly Press* describing the charge of Brackett's Battalion, which ended near a place called Falling Springs:

> No more welcome order could have been given to the tired veterans of his command. With a yell, they swept down the hillside, across a ravine, up the opposite slope, and in a moment were upon them. The enemy were in no mood for retreating, they fought over every foot as they retired and yielded up no vantage ground until its capacities for defense had been tested to the utmost.
>     The charge was a succession of desperate hand-to-hand encounters, which ended only in the death of one or the other party. The wounded Indian, as he lay struggling on the ground, drew the arrow to its head with his teeth when he could no longer use his hands.
>     A mile and a half of this kind of work brought them to the foot of a high Butte, with sides steep as the walls of a house. Here the savages seemed determined to make a stand, but there was no halt. A few shells from a twelve pounder Howitzer which had been busy with others in the center, startled the savages from their fancied security and dismounting the men went at it with a will. Sharpshooters cleared the sides with their carbines and foot by foot the men won their way to the top and sweeping down the opposite side drove the last of the savages to the hills beyond and the fight was over. . . .
>     I have written this in great haste and must ask to be excused for

errors, as I am still unable to mount my horse from the effects of severe wounds.[10]

The butte over which Brackett's Battalion fought after their mounted charge was named by Captain von Minden on his map as "Brackett's Peak."

Sitting Bull gave an account of Brackett's charge, providing a description of the hand-to-hand combat that took place before the battalion dismounted at the foot of the butte:

> Once, when some of our Teton Sioux were skirmishing with the foot soldiers, Brackett's cavalry charged and stopped us. We galloped towards a small hill where some of our Sioux sat mounted and waiting, who then charged the cavalry, who in turn wheeled and retreated on the run. The Sioux horses were fresh and much faster, so we pulled some of the troopers from their saddles, counting coup on them.[11]

Lieutenant G. Merrill Dwelle of the Third Minnesota Battery observed a concentration of Indians gathering behind a hill in tall grass for an ambush against Brackett's charge. Dwelle quickly brought one field piece forward within a few hundred yards of the battalion and fired one twelve-pound case shot into the Indian concentration, driving the Indians into the woods and brush. A dozen more rounds were dropped in the woods on the side of the butte in support of Brackett's Battalion, inflicting many Indian casualties.

Sully's troops came within a half a mile of the village before the women and children rushed back to start packing for evacuation. Most of the Sioux warriors began collecting in a line between the village and soldiers to delay the attack and provide time for their families to escape. The dismounted skirmishers closed their intervals, narrowing the column as Pope's Battery was brought up for a final assault.

The battery began shelling the village with devastating effect, allowing the natives no time to gather their belongings, much less their lodges. The Sioux fled through the village into the cover of the brush and ravines of the Killdeer mountains, exiting out the back side where the terrain was too rugged for the soldiers' pursuit. It was 6:00 P.M. when the troops entered the village. Before sunset, a group of Indians appeared at the summit of one of the hills behind the camp. Four companies of the Eighth Minnesota climbed the hill in pursuit, killing several more before calling off the fight as the Indians fled down the wooded slopes out of reach. With the exception of a few more defiant stragglers, who were chased out of the ravines, the battle was over.

Sully estimated the Sioux losses to be about 150 dead. But there was no way of obtaining an accurate count due to so many of the dead and wounded being borne from the battlefield by the Indians. Brackett found twenty-seven of the Indians dead over the area where his men had fought besides an unknown number who were carried off. Sully's losses were only two killed and ten wounded. Most of the casualties were received by Brackett's Battalion.

Twenty-two-year-old Private Horatio Austin of Company D was killed while dismounted and climbing up the side of the mountain in pursuit of the hostiles. In addition to Eugene Marshall, seven other men in the battalion were wounded: two in Company A, three in Company C, and two in Company D. The battalion lost twenty-two horses as well. Brackett's Battalion also lost one of its bravest and most distinguished men; Orderly Sergeant George Northrup was found dead on the battlefield.

In the charge, Northup raced far ahead of his company to be the first to reach his old enemy. But the legendary "Kit Carson" of the Northwest finally pushed his luck too far. Recognizing an easy target, the Indians swarmed on him before any of his company could reach him. After the battle, he was found with several arrows in his body, one being in the heart, and several bullet wounds. Three days later Sergeant Frederick McCarty, who claimed he was near Northrup when he fell, told Eugene Marshall that Northrup, "charged up to a line of dismounted Indians with his carbine & revolver empty & his sabre in the scabbard." For many years after, the old veterans could not speak about Northrup without their eyes swelling with tears.

That evening, Sully camped his troops on the battlefield in front of the village near a small stream where there was good water for the men and animals. It was a welcome camp for the command as the men, horses, and mules alike were exhausted, hungry, and parched with thirst. Wary of an Indian attack, the soldiers found it nearly impossible to sleep in spite of their exhaustion. Throughout the night shots rang out, disturbing the silence as pickets shot at shadows and imaginary Indians.

The next morning, Sully organized a small expedition to encircle Killdeer Mountain and pick up the Indians' trail. Upon reaching the north side after several miles of marching, Sully found the terrain impossible for the detachment to cross over. As far as the eye could see, the country was cut by deep ravines, filled with timber, with almost perpendicular banks. Sully gave up the pursuit and returned to the village.

Knowing he could do more damage by destroying the Sioux winter supplies than killing a single Indian, Sully ordered the village to be burned. All day the troops worked collecting everything in the camp to be destroyed. Colonel Robert McLaren of the Second Minnesota Cavalry, in charge of the detail, listed in his report the extent of the destruction: "The men gathered into heaps and burned tons of dried buffalo meat packed in buffalo-skin cases, great quantities of dried berries, buffalo robes, tanned buffalo, elk, and antelope skins, household utensils, such as brass and copper kettles, mess pans, etc., riding saddles, dray poles for ponies and dogs."[12]

All of the lodges were brought down, but due to the lack of time, only the poles were burned. It was estimated that more than two hundred tons of supplies and equipment were destroyed. Practically nothing was carried away by the soldiers. Then McLaren ordered that the nearby woods in all directions be burned.

That night Sully and his two brigades retraced their battle path from the mountain and camped about six miles away. As usual, picket posts were placed around the expedition three to four miles out, and as night fell, no fires were allowed in camp. The men of Brackett's Battalion now had time to prepare their two fallen comrades for burial. Under the cover of darkness, the graves for George Northrup and Horatio Austin were dug under the horses' picket line. In silence, without the usual military ceremony, the bodies were positioned in the graves, the dirt replaced, and the horses picketed over the ground. Overnight the horses' hooves would trample the ground leaving no trace of the grave site, preventing the Indians from locating the bodies for the purpose of uncovering and mutilating them.

During the burial, a few Indians managed to sneak in close to one of the other unit camps in an attempt to stampede the horses that were picketed individually outside that camp. After some brief commotion, the horses were saved and the intruders chased off. Tragically, during the alarm, one man of the Sixth Iowa Cavalry was mistaken for an Indian and fatally shot by a picket guard in the darkness near the horses. The next morning two men of the Second Minnesota at one of the outer picket posts were found dead, their bodies pierced with arrows.

# Battle through the Badlands

SULLY'S EXPEDITION arrived back at the Heart River base camp on July 31 during a driving rainstorm, having made a round-trip march of more than 170 miles. That night the thunderstorm stampeded the emigrants' cattle and some of the mules, but all were recovered the next day. The pioneers of the Holmes wagon train were relieved to see the troops return. After Sully's two brigades had left the camp on the twenty-sixth, the small detachment of soldiers and the settlers made preparations for a possible attack on their camp.

Fearing that the Sioux warriors might avoid Sully's column and attack the civilian corral, a line of semicircular-shaped rifle pits were dug along the outer edge of the camp. For extra measure, a "Quaker gun" was produced from a hollowed log tightly wrapped with steel bands. The gun was test fired several times and proved to be workable. The camp was thrown into a frenzy of excitement on at least two nights when the howls of wolves and coyotes pierced the night air. But no hints of an Indian attack came.

After two days of rest, Sully's troops again took up their line of march on the morning of August 3, heading in a westerly direction along the north side of the Heart River with the Holmes wagon train in tow. Sully's Indian scouts knew nothing about the region west of the Yellowstone River. The scouts urged the general to turn the expedition back to Fort Rice, claiming there was no known passage to the Yellowstone and any attempt to reach it would be foolhardy.

But one young scout, a Yankton Sioux, claimed he had hunted in the area with his father a few years earlier and knew a way through. Sully had previously arranged for three shallow-draft steamboats to meet him on the Yellowstone with supplies and was determined to make the rendezvous. Despite doubts expressed by the other guides, Sully put his trust in the young scout and headed west.

On the fifth, the expedition came to the edge of the rolling tableland that provided smooth passage only to be confronted with terrain that put the assembly in utter disbelief. No one was prepared for the spectacle before them. As far as the eye could see to the west, north, and south lay the barren chasm of the Badlands. The awesome view provided a variety of descriptions. Sully, who first described it as, "Hell with the fire put out," wrote in his report to General Pope,

> It was grand, dismal, and majestic. You can imagine a deep basin, 600 feet deep and twenty-five miles in diameter, filled with a number of cones and oven-shaped knolls of all sizes, from twenty feet to several hundred feet high, sometimes by themselves, sometimes piled up into large heaps on top of one another, in all conceivable shapes and confusion. Most of these hills were of a gray clay, but many of a light brick color, of burnt clay; little or no vegetation. Some of the sides of the hills, however, were covered with a few scrub cedars. Viewed in the distance at sunset it looked exactly like the ruins of an ancient city.[1]

In a letter to the *St. Paul Press,* Eugene Marshall wrote,

> we found ourselves on the edge of a country the very sight of which caused a shudder of apprehension in every man in the command and which beggars description. From the high ground, to the right and left and in front rose a succession of hills, sharp as wheat stocks of our Minnesota farmers, thicker than the shocks of grain upon their fields in harvest. It was a perfect labyrinth to which there seemed no outlet and where no eye could trace out a path for a man to walk, much less for passage of loaded wagons. I can assure you that this was not a cheerful camp.[2]

Camping for the night, Sully began to assess the situation. He was tempted to turn back to Fort Rice, but after taking an inventory of his rations for the troops, he discovered the commissary officer at Fort Rice had made an error in distribution. There were only enough rations for six more days. Sully was thus compelled to trust a single Indian scout and march for the Yellowstone, bringing his wounded and the Holmes wagon train with him and hoping the steamboats would be waiting with supplies. Sully ordered the bread ration to be reduced to one-third and the rest to one-half.

The next morning the expedition descended into the canyon over a long land ramp, as there appeared to be no other entrance without making a detour. The young scout seemed to know his business. But soon a detail of solders with picks and shovels were sent to the front to clear the road or to virtually make a road. The "pioneers," as they were called, filled in holes and gullies and carved away the sides of buttes clearing the way for the wagons. Entering the Badlands, the expedition was greeted by wonders few white people had laid eyes on before. Sully wrote,

> we marched through a most wonderful and interesting country. It was covered with pieces of petrified wood, and on the tops of some of the hills we found petrified stumps of trees, the remains of a great forest. In some cases these trees were sixteen to eighteen feet in diameter. Large quantities of iron ore, lava, and impressions in the rocks of leaves of a size and shape not known to any of us. [3]

By nightfall, the three-mile-long column of mounted soldiers, wagons, and cattle reached the Little Missouri River. The drought had reduced the wide river to a narrow trickle, but it was enough to provide relief for everyone. For the animals, however, there was barely enough grazing vegetation along the banks to sustain them.

Sully planned to rest for a day, a Sunday, on the Little Missouri. That morning a detail of "pioneers" with an escort of four companies was sent ahead to clear a trail. Sully wrote, "Having dug our way down to this point it was now necessary to dig our way out." But the expedition's day of rest was cut short. In the afternoon a party of Indians crept into camp, firing on the soldiers and managing to stampede some of the horses. Most of the horses were recovered, but it was now clear that the expedition could not remain in one place for even a day.

Immediately Sully broke camp and moved the expedition three miles up river where a location for a defense and grass for grazing was found to be more suitable. After cutting three miles of road, the advance party also came under attack and was forced to retreat, rejoining the expedition at its new camp. The hostiles, following the pioneer party, fired into the camp from a high bluff on the opposite bank. A few rounds from the artillery scattered them and, with the exception of some light picket firing, the trouble subsided for the night.

"I now knew I had come upon the Indians I fought about a week ago," Sully wrote, " . . . and in the worst possible section of country I could possibly wish to encounter an enemy." Eugene Marshall continued to carry out most of his duties as sergeant major. But because of his wounds, he was confined to an ambulance wagon while on the march. It was probably the aggravation of his wounds that prevented him from writing about the Indian fighting. But he still managed to make a note about the terrain in his diary as the march resumed the next day:

> We have marched today nearly every point of [the] compass amongst hills & buttes innumerable, yet by winding amongst them have found a road practicable for the wagons with but very little work, but have not made over eight miles. I do not believe that the counterpart of that country exists any where else on earth.[4]

It was the Sans Arc Sioux who discovered the expedition struggling through the Badlands. When they contacted the Hunkpapa camp, Sitting Bull was asked to join them in attacking Sully. Sitting Bull recalled,

> I smoked the war pipe, agreeing to join the Sans Arcs in fighting the soldiers and the Hunkpapa moved to the Sans Arc camp. Next day we met the soldiers at the crossing on the Little Missouri and the battle began at this point. In this badland country the whites were at a great disadvantage even though they had about two thousand men. The wagons could barely be dragged over this flat topped butte country that was so badly cut up. There was little water, men and horses suffered greatly. Many horses and mules starved and died in these badlands. The soldiers were scattered out for miles, retreating as fast as possible under these adverse conditions. We pushed after them all day and night and shots were exchanged whenever groups of Indians and soldiers came into contact with each other.[5]

Other bands of Indians arrived from all directions to take advantage of the expedition's entrapped situation. In his letter to the *Press* a few days later Marshall wrote, "The number of Indians has been variously estimated at from one to four thousand. All I can say is that they completely surrounded our command and could be seen in great numbers on every hilltop; their line could not have been less than ten miles long."[6]

For two days, after leaving the Little Missouri, the soldiers dug and fought their way through the drought-stricken gorge. Each day the two brigades traded duties taking the advance or the rear and guarding the flanks of the supply wagons and the emigrant wagon train. From ravines, behind hills, and on top of buttes, Indian attacks came from all directions. Cavalrymen were often dismounted to charge Indian formations on higher ground.

Again the artillery was busy. It was proving to be the expedition's greatest strength. Pope's and Jones's batteries, with great effect, kept most of the hostiles from attacking in large numbers. At times the warriors gathered in numbers on high ground so close to the artillery that the guns had to be run up on knolls with the trails resting down the slope in order for the pieces to be elevated enough to make an accurate shot.

Some of the heaviest fighting took place at the site of a small pond, now a mud hole, and a spring that provided the only water since leaving the Little Missouri. It was during this second day of fighting that Sully nearly lost his only guide through the Badlands. The Yankton scout was severely wounded, becoming too weak to give directions. Placed in a wagon at the head of the column, the young man was propped up by two others enabling him to spot landmarks, using his strength to raise his hand and point the way.

At night the attacks were less fierce but enough to keep the pickets busy. The troops slept on their arms with no shelters while many of the horses remained saddled. Gunfire erupted inside the camp on more than one night, as well as hand-to-hand fighting among the horses at the picket lines as Indians crept in to steal horses. But each time the warriors were killed or driven off.

After a day of protecting the rear of the column and the "Idaho train," the First Brigade took the advance on the ninth, experiencing much of the same kind of action as the Second Brigade had the previous day. Marshall wrote in his letter to the *Press,*

> this time it was the advance of the 1st Brigade under command of Major Brackett which had the brunt of the fight, but steadily the column advanced only halting when necessary to pour a withering fire upon the savages and before night, broken spirited and subdued, they left us to ourselves and followed the trail of their retreating families, which could be seen before us plain as a wagon road and half a mile broad.[7]

In his report to the general, Brackett described his actions of the ninth.

I received orders to proceed to the front with Company C of my battalion and one section of the Prairie battery, under command of Captain Pope, which order I carried into execution at once. Dismounting two platoons and deploying them as skirmishers, under command of Lieutenant Neely, I ordered Captain Shelley with the remainder of the company to support the battery. The enemy could be seen in great numbers on every side, and seemed determined to resist our progress, but the excellent practice of Captain Pope's howitzers dispersed them with loss and frustrated every attempt to rally for an attack. A running fight was kept up until about 2 PM, when the Indians disappeared. From the nature of the ground and the distance which the savages maintained, I am unable to estimate their loss, which must have been heavy. The remaining three companies of my battalion marched in the usual order on the left of the first Brigade, under command of Captain Barton, of Company D. Early in the day they were much annoyed by the Indians, and some severe skirmishing ensued. One man of Company D becoming separated from his command had his horse wounded by a bullet, but escaped, after killing or severely wounding two Indians. No other loss was sustained.[8]

In Sully's report he stated, "the last we saw of the Indians was a cloud of dust some six or eight miles off, running as fast as they could. They were better mounted than we were."

Emerging from the Badlands, the expedition reached open country where Sully found the site of the abandoned Indian camp. He reported, "From the size of their camp, or rather bivouac, for they had pitched no lodges, I should judge all the Indians in the country had assembled there. The space they occupied was over one mile long and half a mile wide."[9]

Sully also learned the expedition had engaged a greater number of tribes than at Killdeer Mountain: "The same Indians I fought before were engaged, besides Cheyennes, Brules, Minneconjous, and others from the south."

It was impossible to determine the number of Indian casualties sustained during the Badlands fight. As always the Indians made every effort while fighting to carry their dead and wounded away. Sully estimated one hundred to three hundred killed and a larger number wounded. Due to the nature of the battle, military casualties were much larger in this engagement. Nine men were killed and about a hundred wounded. There were no known casualties in Brackett's Battalion.

The march through the Badlands continued to take a toll on the animals as well. The drought-stricken terrain, void of vegetation and water, caused several horses, mules, oxen, and cattle to give out, leaving a trail of animal carcasses and abandoned wagons. At times during the Indian fighting, the rear guard was prevented from shooting some of the suffering animals when some of the women from the emigrant train unknowingly placed themselves in the line of fire while they tried to coax failing cattle and oxen with tufts of grass. Resuming the march on the open plain, the column renewed its battle against nature.

Entering Montana Territory the expedition found no relief from the land. What little grass there may have been was eaten off by buffalo and grasshoppers. Creek beds were dry and the small ponds of water found were alkaline, further deteriorating the condition of the soldiers, emigrants, and animals. In his letter to the *Press,* Marshall wrote, "One day we marched thirty-five miles over a country incapable of supporting any living thing. The grass there was absolutely none, horses and mules fell dead by the way. Men parched with thirst and mad from alkali water staggered along leading the horses which could no longer carry them."[10]

On August 12, after three days of dreadful marching from the Badlands, one of the scouts from the advance party returned to the column with a chip of wood in his hand. After showing it to General Sully, the scout rode along the column displaying the item. It was a piece of the hull from one of the steamers waiting on the Yellowstone River. Up to this time the soldiers and emigrants were unable to utter any sounds from their parched throats and swollen tongues. But upon the sight of the wood chip, everyone managed to let out a cheer. Marshall wrote, "None but men who have been in the like circumstances can imagine the glad shout which went up from a thousand throats when on the evening of August 12th we saw the Yellowstone and smoke from two steamboats."[11]

The organized column of cavalrymen and emigrants broke, resulting in a mad dash for the river. The animals had to be restrained from plunging into the rushing water for fear of drowning or overdrinking.

But many of the men leaped into the water in uncontrolled excitement. Waiting at the riverbank were the steamers *Alone* and *Chippewa Falls,* the first steamers to ascend the Yellowstone. The two shallow-draft riverboats were loaded with about one hundred tons of much-needed supplies. The third boat, the *Island City,* carrying nearly all the forage and corn for the animals, had struck a snag and sunk on the Missouri just short of the Yellowstone.

It was a stroke of luck that Sully's expedition reached the Yellowstone at the point where the steamers had landed. Sully had intended to reach the river farther upstream, closer to the Powder River where he would establish a new post. The riverboats carried supplies and material for the post's construction. But the heavily laden steamers, due to the decreasing water level, were forced to stop where they were. Sully's Indian guide led the expedition on the easiest and shortest route through the Badlands bringing the column, by fate, to the steamers.

Here again, Sully was forced to decide how the expedition would complete its mission. Low water on the Yellowstone prevented the steamers from continuing farther upriver. Plus, without feed, the health of the animals would improve little. Sully was compelled to abandon his trek to the Powder River. The best route now was to turn north to Fort Union at the mouth of the Yellowstone on the upper Missouri and from there return to Fort Rice.

The best ground for the march to Fort Union was on the west side of the Yellowstone. Rather than camping for the night, the expedition immediately began crossing the river. All of the supplies were unloaded from the wagons and ferried across by the steamers. Wagons were pulled across the shallow river by the teams, but the swift river current still made the crossing treacherous. After two days, the crossing was completed but not without loss. Two cavalrymen were drowned on the thirteenth. The next day, two men from the Holmes wagon train drowned while herding the cattle across. Additionally there was the loss of a few animals and wagons from both parties.

Against the general's advice, many of the miners now believed they could leave the protection of the military and head west for the goldfields. Unable to decide on what route to take, the emigrant train split up into three groups, each setting out on different courses. One larger group remained with the military until reaching Fort Union.

Because grazing was still sparse, Sully scattered his command over several miles along the river so the animals would not have to compete for forage. For three days the expedition rested before beginning a one-day march to Fort Union. As they lay in camp, the troops filled themselves with fresh meat from an abundance of buffalo, elk, and blacktail deer that roamed nearby. The men also found berries and choke cherries, despite the desertlike conditions. An improved diet helped relieve the men of their dysentery.

On the seventeenth, the expedition arrived on the bank of the Missouri River, opposite Fort Union, a few miles upstream from the mouth of the Yellowstone. Here the river, with a swift current and quicksand bottom, proved to be even more dangerous for a crossing. The animals were herded across over shallow sandbars, losing a few in the process. The wagons were dismantled and ferried across on the steamers. It took three days to complete the task with the loss of one man.

After crossing over, a party of Crow Indians arrived at Sully's headquarters claiming they had been chased by a large band of Sioux. Brackett's Battalion with a section of Pope's battery was ordered out during the night to hunt the warriors down, only to find that the Crows were probably running from a cloud of dust kicked up by a large herd of buffalo.

The expedition made camp near the fort as the troops began preparing for the long march back to their base camp. Established in 1830 by the American Fur Company, Fort Union had been a thriving trading post with friendly Indians, mostly enemies of the Sioux. Now in its declining days, the fort was found to be deteriorating, but the company still managed to keep up a respectable business. Marshall, always recording in his diary what he saw, overestimated the fort's dimensions by nearly twice the actual size:

> It is a strong stockade about four hundred feet square with two stone bastions two stories high at opposite angles. There are a few white men kept here by the fur company. One company of the 30th Wisc. is here and there are a very few Indians, Crows. Apparently there is a huge business done here in furs.[12]

As the Northwestern Indian Expedition began to gather for its march, the remainder of the Holmes wagon train bid their farewells before starting out on a previously established trail to the Idaho goldfields. Marshall wrote, "The Idaho emigrants sent a deputation to wait on Major Brackett, thanking him for his kind treatment of them while on the march and the uniform courtesy of his command. It took the Major by surprise as he was not aware that he had done anything for them."[13]

Later it was learned that the wagon train had made off with several firearms, ammunition, horses, mules, and oxen from the military expedition. Sully dispatched a company of the Dakota Cavalry in pursuit of the train to recover the property, as well as apprehend a few deserters from the expedition who had fled with them. But the miners had too much of a head start. The detail returned empty-handed.

That portion of the Holmes expedition arrived at Fort Benton in mid-September without incident. From there the miners and settlers scattered to various mining camps and boomtowns where they pursued a variety of business endeavors, most of all gold prospecting. One of their numbers would name the Helena settlement.

Sully's command began its return march to Fort Rice on August 22. On the twenty-eighth the column stopped near Fort Berthold for two days' rest while Sully held conferences with the peaceful Indians camped nearby. The original fort was established by the American Fur Company in 1845 near the river. It had maintained a thriving trade with the friendly Gros Ventre, Mandan, and Ree Indians, enemies of the Sioux. By 1862 the company took over a competitor's fort located closer to the Indian villages, renaming it Fort Berthold. The original stockade was attacked and destroyed by the Sioux on Christmas Eve of 1862.

Eugene Marshall was recovering well from his wounds. But he would never again wear a saber belt or carry a side arm because of the wounds' lingering irritation. As usual he recorded his observations of the local natives and their village:

The Mandans are the best looking of all the Indians we have seen. They have very large fields of corn below here & I saw many small hay stacks, both of which show them to be industrious. They were dressed in their best today, & some of them made really a fine appearance with their fringed legin[g]s and jackets of white antelope skin; many of them worked in very pretty figures with beads & colored porcupine quills. . . .

One old grey headed fellow whose eagle feathers denoted many scalps, after I had been pointed out to him as having been wounded by the Sioux, came up to me and shook hands as if he recognized some bond of fellowship between us. . . .

There are at least two thousand in all. They live in long lodges of poles covered with dirt, circular in form. . . . All is covered with dirt except a round hold in the center through which the smoke escapes from an open fire. . . . The ponies are kept in the same room with the family. . . . There can not be less than six or eight hundred acres of corn. . . . The dogs were at work bringing in corn about a bushel to a dog on two poles crossed on his back & dragging on the ground behind.[14]

After learning about a hostile Sioux camp to the northeast, the expedition left Fort Berthold on September 1 to investigate the possible threat. After a day of marching, Sully arrived at the site of the abandoned camp from which the Sioux appeared to be fleeing for the British territory. Aware of the condition of the horses and other animals, Sully decided not to pursue the band further. The expedition turned back to the Missouri River and resumed the march to Fort Rice.

Buffalo herds in numbers of several hundred to several thousand were an ever-present source of fresh meat for the troops. The day the command left Fort Berthold, Marshall wrote, "This has been a great day for buffalo. All that we have seen were as nothing compared to what we have seen today. I estimate that I saw ten thousand at once." But at times the herds were more of a threat than an advantage. Every blade of grass was consumed by the buffalo, leaving nothing for the animals of the command. At some camps, nearby lakes were found to be fouled by buffalo manure, "But coffee was made anyway."

The giant herds were also a direct threat to the troops themselves. At several camps the supply wagons were corralled around the various unit camps, instead of in the center as usual, to protect the troops from buffalo stampedes. But these measures sometimes proved to be too little against a massive herd startled by a bugler's call or blinded by their own dust cloud on the run to a nearby watering hole. Such stampedes would demolish a camp in seconds. "As far as the vision extended, the plain was almost black with the moving, thundering mass," recalled one man of the Eighth Minnesota Regiment.

On September 9, the command reached Fort Rice, making camp on the opposite bank. There was no need for the expedition to cross over to the fort's side of the river. The troops would be heading home soon to Minnesota or Sioux City, Iowa, for the winter. What lay ahead for them in the following year was yet unknown. During a year of severe drought, the campaign proved not to be the "pleasure trip" Eugene Marshall predicted it would be. On the surface, the 1864 Northwestern Indian Expedition appeared to be over. But when they arrived at Fort Rice, General Sully learned that there was one more mission in store for them.

# Captain Fisk's Perilous Wagon Train

WHEN THE FIRST BRIGADE of the Northwestern Indian expedition left Fort Sully on June 26, Sergeant Willoughby Wells of Brackett's Battalion, Company B, was left behind. He was to take charge of a detail of cavalrymen for the protection of government freight awaiting transport to the various posts upriver. Low water level on the Missouri River compelled all upbound streamers to unload a portion of their cargo at Fort Sully. After making deliveries to Fort Rice, Fort Berthold, or Fort Union, the steamers would return for the remainder of the freight to make a second delivery. Sergeant Wells with his guard detail accompanied the last of the reloaded freight upriver, arriving at Fort Rice during the first week of August.

A few days later, an emigrant wagon train from Minnesota led by Captain James L. Fisk, destined for the Idaho goldfields, arrived at the fort. The train was accompanied by a cavalry contingent of about fifty troops under orders to escort the emigrants only as far as the Missouri River in Dakota Territory. From there it was believed the wagon train would connect with General Sully's expedition and then continue west to the Yellowstone River. But to Captain Fisk's dismay, Sully's troops, along with the Holmes wagon train, had long since departed.

Believing he could follow Sully's trail west, Fisk tried to use his military rank to order the escort to continue on with him as far as the Yellowstone. Pointing out that their horses were too weak from the long march across the dry plains and that the captain could not override their orders, given to them by a superior officer, the detail refused.

In need of a new escort, Fisk turned to the fort commander, Colonel Daniel J. Dill, who, he found, had little more to offer. The troops of the Thirtieth Wisconsin were there to construct and garrison the fort, making them unavailable for escort duty. The only cavalrymen on hand were those too ill to march with Sully's expedition. And the few cavalry horses at the post had been declared unfit for a long march.

Colonel Dill called upon the troops in the convalescent camp to volunteer for the escort duty. Fisk was looking for at least fifty men but was able to obtain only forty-five volunteers, a few from each of the units in Sully's command, who seemed reasonably fit for duty. However, Fisk had brought with him a twelve-pound mountain howitzer that he obtained at Fort Snelling. Although having a limited supply of canister shot and powder for the gun, Fisk was confident he was armed well enough to ward off any possible Indian attack. Lieutenant DeWitt Smith was placed in command of the escort with the thirty-one-year-old Sergeant Wells, a veteran of two years in the South, as second in charge. After the best of the jaded horses were selected for the escort, the Fisk wagon train left Fort Rice following Sully's trail west along the Cannonball River.

James Fisk had enlisted as a private with the Third Minnesota Infantry in the fall of 1861. In the spring of the following year, he was appointed as assistant quartermaster in the volunteer staff corps with the rank of captain. His real assignment was to organize overland migration to the gold region in Idaho Territory.

The Federal government was encouraging settlement of the western gold mining regions in order to acquire the precious metal to help finance the war against the South. Commissioned by the government, Fisk possessed the skills to help lead the expansion from Minnesota. In 1862, Captain Fisk led his first overland wagon train to the Idaho goldfields from Minnesota. The success of the expedition led Fisk to a second crossing in the summer of 1863. He then followed the previous year's trail from northern Minnesota, across northern Dakota Territory above the Missouri River.

With two successful crossings to his credit, the young captain began making preparations during the winter of 1863–64 for a third crossing, which would begin in the spring. Fisk, twenty-eight years old, was an energetic and persuasive recruiter. He lectured to large audiences in town halls, churches, and in the streets. With a bugle in one hand and gold nuggets in the other, Fisk captivated prospective gold seekers and settlers all across the northern states.

Fisk believed that a more direct southern route to the mining camps, originating from southern Minnesota, would reduce the traveling distance by several hundred miles. During a visit to the White House, he convinced President Abraham Lincoln that he, Fisk, could blaze the trail for the new southern road. But the U.S. Congress was unwilling to provide funding for such a project. Instead, Fisk was provided ten thousand dollars for the protection of immigration over the old northern trail. The War Department supported the plan by placing Fisk under orders to use the established route.

But Captain Fisk was a volunteer officer with little motivation to follow army policy to the letter. He still believed that a southern route to Idaho Territory would reduce traveling distance and was determined to prove it. He was even more resolved to take the short cut when he learned Thomas Holmes, who also led settlers to the goldfields in 1862, had left Minnesota with his wagon train, ahead of Fisk, with the Second Brigade of the Northwestern Indian Expedition.

Fisk was delayed in Washington as he waited for Congress to make a decision on the proposed construction of a southern road. By the time he had returned to St. Paul, the Holmes party had been on the trail for more than a week. It then took Fisk nearly a month to organize his wagon train.

The expedition, consisting of a mixture of about eighty ox-drawn wagons and Red River carts and some 170 men, women, and children, assembled at Fort Ridgely. It was not until July 23 that the Fisk wagon train finally got under way. Unaware that Fisk was under orders to use the northern trail, General Sibley provided Fisk with a cavalry escort of fifty men as far as the Missouri River. The captain, with his usual optimism, assumed that the Holmes expedition would be waiting for him somewhere along the way.

Starting up the Minnesota River Valley, the wagon train turned west at Big Stone Lake into Dakota Territory. Fisk intended to head due west to cross the Missouri. But after a few days out, he realized that General Sully's troops and the Holmes train had moved north to Fort Rice. The captain was obliged to steer his course to the fort where he expected to catch up with Holmes and Sully. Although disappointed to find neither party at the fort, Fisk collected his less-than-healthy escort and set out on August 23 to follow Sully's trail along the Cannonball.

He knew Sully was marching for the Yellowstone River. Although the route was slightly farther north than what Fisk had planned, he thought that following Sully would be just as good. Believing Sully had swept all hostile Sioux in his path away from the trail, Fisk was unconcerned about warnings of a possible attack on his lightly escorted train. Because the miners were well armed and they had the mountain howitzer, the party was confident they could repel any attack. However, during the first night out after leaving Fort Rice, five of the soldiers deserted the expedition and returned to the fort, leaving only forty to guard the train.

After about eight miles Captain Fisk found that Sully's trail had curiously turned north, well away from the intended direction. Determined to pioneer a more direct route, Fisk turned the wagon train to the southwest knowing he was now on his own. A few of the train's staff members were veterans of the 1863 expedition but had no knowledge of this relatively unexplored region. One of his scouts was thirty-nine-year-old Jefferson Dilts, once a corporal with the First Minnesota Mounted Rangers.

Lieutenant Smith, commanding the escort, was from the Nebraska company of the First Dakota Cavalry, awaiting a decision from the War Department about the proceedings of a court martial against him. Willoughby Wells, several years later, recorded his experience with the Fisk wagon train. He recalled the mood of the lieutenant and his own role in the expedition:

> He was the only cavalry officer at Fort Rice, and was sent in command of the escort as a case of emergency. He felt his degradation deeply and took little interest in what was going on around us; and I soon discovered that he always looked to me for counsel regarding the welfare of our men, and never gave us an order without a suggestion from me, as I was the only noncommissioned officer in the company.[1]

Sundays were observed as a day of rest, allowing the emigrants to make repairs on the wagons and rest the animals. Fisk organized activities of amusement during the rest stops to relieve the boredom. During the first Sunday, the captain arranged a shooting contest among the miners, nearly all of whom were armed with "globe-sighted" rifles. Wells recalled,

> The following Sunday he invited the best shot from among the soldiers with army guns to compete with the best shot from the train men for a prize of ten dollars. The result was that I defeated his champion and walked off with the prize. I always thought he gave it with some reluctance, as he felt sure that an army rifle stood no chance with the high priced guns of the members of his expedition.[2]

Wells used the ten dollars to purchase tobacco, which he shared with the rest of the escort.

The expedition eventually turned its course in a more westerly direction. Here the terrain gradually changed from gently rolling prairie with few obstacles to become flat and open. A majority of the cavalry escort rode well ahead of the wagons, stopping every so often to rest, allowing the slow moving ox teams to catch up. The remainder of the escort followed the train as the rear guard.

In the late afternoon of September 2, as Sergeant Wells and the advance party rested, Wells looked back at the long string of wagons and noticed an odd formation of riders near the rear creating some commotion. Seeing that the last two wagons and the rear guard had lagged far behind after one of the wagons overturned at a creek crossing, his worst fears were realized—an Indian attack:

> We immediately wheeled, put spurs to our horses and hastened to protect the rear of the train from attack, and get between the train and the hostile red men. On reaching the [rear] we found that the Indians had succeeded in cutting off our rear guard of nine men and two wagons, each with three yokes of oxen. One of these wagons was loaded with saloon supplies which the Indians proceeded to enjoy, and the other carried a mixed load of freight, among the articles there being some ammunition and a few rifles which were at once appropriated by these wards of Uncle Sam.[3]

It was Sitting Bull's band of Hunkpapa Sioux who met the wagon train, by coincidence, while moving their camp to the southern hunting grounds after their fight with General Sully's expedition in the Badlands. Riding with the rear guard, Corporal Thomas Williamson of the Sixth Iowa Cavalry spotted the approaching Indians and turned to fend off their advances, while the rest of the soldiers prepared for a defense. One warrior rode out and met the corporal, pulling Williamson and himself to the ground. As the two struggled in a hand-to-hand fight, a second warrior arrived to join in. Williamson managed to fight off his attackers. He severely wounded one with a blow from the gun he had pulled from the second Indian, as he received several strikes himself from a war club and a knife.

Then Sitting Bull, believing his party had only happened onto a small detachment from Sully's command, galloped to the scene to help the two warriors who had lost their fight against Williamson. Leaning over the side of his horse, he shot an arrow into the corporal's back but still with little effect. Williamson turned and fired his revolver, shooting the chief in the hip. Sitting Bull rode back to his group with a flesh wound and remained in camp for the duration of the encounter. Williamson remounted his horse and returned to the wagon train to report to Captain Fisk about the situation. Fisk described the corporal in his report.

> He sat straight up in his saddle as he rode up to me, while he had nine different cuts from Tomahawks, knives and war clubs, besides arrows sticking deep in his back and sides. Blood streamed from his head and body and was dripping down his horse's sides.[4]

With the help of some of the men from the wagon train, the cavalrymen skirmished with a band of about sixty Sioux who were proceeding to loot the two captured wagons. After two hours of fighting, the attackers were driven off but not before they were able to take with them about two thousand rounds of ammunition and several Sharps carbines along with various other supplies.

The expedition suffered a high number of casualties in the attack. Nine cavalrymen and civilians were killed along with four wounded. Three of the men killed in the rear guard were from the Eighth Minnesota. Two more were from Brackett's Battalion—twenty-one-year-old Ernest Hoffinaster of Company A and William Chase, also twenty-one, of Company D. Among the wounded was the train's signal scout, Jefferson Dilts, found with three arrows in his body and three dead Sioux warriors sprawled around him.

After the attack, with several dead Indians left at the scene, the wagons were corralled in a defensive position. The soldiers and civilians killed in the attack were buried with military honors inside the corral. No assaults were made on the camp that night. Instead, a violent thunderstorm followed by sheets of rain, lasting several hours, kept everyone on edge. In the morning the animals were found standing in two feet of water.

The wagon train started out again that morning, but this time in a shortened column of four wagons abreast. The Indians reappeared to resume the attack at long range. Following a frustrating day-long running skirmish with the loss of several good oxen, cattle, and horses, the train corralled for the night after advancing nine miles. As the teams were being unhitched, the warriors collected in large numbers to the right and rear of the corral for what appeared to be the makings of a general assault. For the first time, the light mountain howitzer was placed in position. One shot from the gun was sufficient to scatter the threatening formation, allowing for a peaceful night.

Knowing the Indians would pounce on anything of value left behind, Fisk's train again resumed its march the next morning leaving behind a box of hardtack soaked in poison. Fisk did not agree that the tactic would be to their benefit but did nothing to stop it. The bread was soon found and quickly consumed by the hungry Sioux warriors who, now numbering about three hundred, renewed their attack more boldly than before.

This time the train advanced only three miles before Lieutenant Smith realized that the enemy was about to make an all-out attack. The wagons halted and started to corral once again. "This was a little sooner than the Indians were fully prepared for," Wells recalled.

> They noticed what we were doing and a number tried to head us off, and before the teams were fairly loosened from the wagons or the train corralled, arrows began to light within a few feet of us. The leader of the Indians had a good rifle and could use it skillfully and was daring enough to come close enough to be easily recognized. He was soon sent, however, to the Happy Hunting Ground, some claiming it was a shot from their gun; and others having the audacity to say it was a chunk of lead from my rifle. I never disputed it; however, I presume it was due more to my accidental success the previous Sunday than to any other reason.[5]

After the loss of their apparent leader, the warriors withdrew for the day but remained visible in the distance. Meanwhile the emigrants and soldiers celebrated. Wells remembered, "a cheer went up from within our lines, and soon there was quite a gathering around one of the emigrants, an old Irishman and an old sport, who had a pail and with a tin cup was serving whiskey to the entire company."[6]

Captain Fisk was alerted to the matter before the men turned into "uncontrollable citizens, as well as soldiers." A Mr. McCarthy, who was hauling saloon supplies to the mines, was promptly stopped, "but a few crawled under the wagons for an afternoon nap."

Fisk with his staff plus Lieutenant Smith and Sergeant Wells began to assess their situation. Surrounded by a superior number of hostile Sioux with two hundred miles of trail between them and Fort Rice in a region little known to white men, the emigrants and soldiers appeared to be in a helpless predicament. After meeting for several hours, the party agreed it would be too hazardous to attempt any further travel. They now looked for a way to be rescued. It was decided that either Lieutenant Smith or Sergeant Wells would lead a detail of fourteen volunteers from the escort back to Fort Rice for help. According to Wells, "The Lieutenant gave me the [choice] of going or remaining. I knew he was desirous of going, as he looked upon this as a chance for influencing the military authorities at Washington, hence I declined to choose and left the choice to him. Lieut. Smith chose to go for reinforcements, and arrangements were made for an immediate start."[7]

The soldiers knew that the trip would be nearly suicidal. But Smith still had no trouble finding fourteen volunteers. Each of the men bid farewell to someone they had acquired a friendship with during the trip. No one was certain they would get past the Indians much less get as far as the fort. Willoughby Wells also gave his best wishes to a friend:

> A young man, John Doudney, whose acquaintance I had made that summer, and hailing from that part of Iowa where my family had taken refuge after the Sioux uprising in 1862, in taking my hand said, "Sergeant Wells, if we never reach Fort Rice, and you are saved, you can tell them of our last service."[8]

After the best of the fatigued horses were selected, their hoofs wrapped with cloth to muffle them, and a small amount of jerked buffalo meat for rations issued to the detail, Smith's message riders left the camp before midnight under the cover of a threatening, misty night. With the rest of their gear muffled as well, the riders were soon out of hearing and out of sight.

In the morning, it appeared that the Sioux were out of sight for a while. The cattle were allowed to graze outside the corral while the emigrants continued to fortify their position with earthworks. Later, the settler's plows were brought out to turn over the prairie sod, which was then placed on the earthworks. The result of this quick labor was a sod wall, two feet thick and six feet high, encircling most of the camp. On the west side were two semicircle rifle pits commanding the low ground in front of them.

One of the men who was watching over the grazing stock outside the corral found several dead Indians lying on the prairie, their corpses half eaten by wolves. It appeared that the poisoned food left at the previous camp was having the intended effect. It was later learned that approximately twenty-five Indians had perished from the bad bread.

That morning a group of Indians, keeping a safe distance from the corral, surveyed the area. They soon found the tracks of the message riders leading away from the camp. Realizing what had gotten by them, a detail from the Sioux immediately gave chase down the trail to stop Smith and his men. As the miners watched from their entrenched camp, they realized the extent of their peril if Lieutenant Smith and his men were caught.

Later that day a large body of Sioux gathered in full view of the camp some distance away. Three riders emerged from the group with a white flag attached to a makeshift staff that they planted in the ground between themselves and the walled camp. A detail was ordered out of the corral to investigate, finding at the place of the flag a letter wedged in a stick. The letter was from a white woman named Fanny Kelly who was being held captive by the Sioux. She had been captured in July after an attack on another wagon train west of Fort Laramie.

Kelly was instructed by her captors to relay their demands. For her release and safe passage of the wagon train, the Sioux demanded provisions of food, gunpowder, and forty head of cattle. But Kelly added a message of her own as well, knowing the Indians would not understand the writing. While pleading for her rescue, she warned Captain Fisk that the Indians could not be trusted and would probably attack the train again in the Badlands where the emigrants would be less able to defend themselves. Kelly also unknowingly hinted at the poisoned hardtack by writing, "They had many killed by the goods they brought into camp."

Fisk was not about to give into the Indians' demands easily. For two days he negotiated with the band through messages between himself and Fanny Kelly and, eventually, through negotiators from his staff who met with the Indians in person. Fisk made it clear that he would not hand over weapons or gunpowder and that he was fully capable of defending against any attack. But he knew that after the loss of ammunition during the first attack, the train could not hold out against a prolonged siege.

Finally Fisk had a team of two horses hitched to a wagon loaded with flour, sugar, coffee, and other supplies with a third horse tied to the wagon. The entire offering was driven to the negotiation site where Kelly was expected to be released. But the Indians refused. Soon the Hunkpapa band left the area, only to be seen on occasion in small numbers in the distance.

Meanwhile, Lieutenant Smith and his message party hurried to Fort Rice completely unharassed. Traveling day and night, the men and horses grew tired and eventually lost the wagon trail. While keeping a correct course, the party traveled parallel with the original trail, relocating it later on. There the men made a startling discovery. The tracks of the Indian ponies were found on the trail heading in the same direction and moving at a quick pace. It appeared that the Sioux party, sent to run down the messengers, had bypassed Smith and his men after they had wandered off the trail. Unable to track down Smith, the warriors returned to their camp with the news that Fisk's wagon train might soon be met by a rescue party.

A few miles from the fort, one of the soldiers' horses gave out. For the rest of the journey the men took turns running on foot. On September 7, Smith and his men arrived at Fort Rice after covering the two-hundred-mile trek in two and a half days. The next day, General Sully, after arriving at the fort a day ahead of his two brigades, learned about Captain Fisk's situation. Sully was furious about the news.

On the ninth, Sully's troops reached their camp opposite the fort. Three months of marching through a drought-stricken, hostile territory, engaging in two battles with the Sioux and losing several horses, mules, and oxen along the way, had left Sully's command in an exhausted state. But the general could not abandon the women and children of the wagon train.

Placing part of the responsibility on Colonel Dill for allowing Fisk to continue on with a light escort, Sully ordered Dill to take command of a rescue party. The detail, composed of mounted and dismounted troops, consisted of three companies of Colonel Dill's Thirtieth Wisconsin, two companies of the Eighth Minnesota, and one company of the Seventh Iowa Cavalry, all dismounted, with a mounted force of one hundred men each of Brackett's Battalion, the Second Minnesota Cavalry, and the Sixth Iowa Cavalry on the best of the horses, accompanied by two howitzers from Pope's Battery. It took the entire day of the tenth to ferry the troops across the river to the fort side. Early the next morning the rescue party started out with the mounted troops taking the lead.

At the emigrant's sod fortified corral, Fisk became aware that the watchful Indians had become much less of a threat. Able to move around the vicinity more freely, Fisk led scouting parties to the west to survey a route he now believed he could pursue without trouble. A clear spring was found about one-half mile away that provided good water for the people and animals. Five miles to the west, the scouts found a branch of the Little Missouri River where there was a well-wooded area and plenty of grass for grazing. In his report, Fisk claimed he had found the clear passage he was looking for that would take him into Montana Territory and beyond—to the goldfields. In reality the treacherous Badlands, about fifteen miles distant, still lay ahead.

Fisk tried to persuade the emigrants and his escort to break camp and resume their course west. But most of them refused, insisting on waiting for a rescue party to take them back to Fort Rice or provide a stronger escort for the remainder of the journey. For Fisk there was no turning back.

On September 8, the two wounded cavalrymen of the Sixth Iowa, Marma Betts and Thomas Williamson, who had wounded Sitting Bull, died. On the nineteenth the expedition's signal scout, Jefferson Dilts, died after sixteen days of suffering. By this time the settlers had all but given up hope that Lieutenant Smith and his men had ever reached Fort Rice. But on the morning of the twentieth, their fears were laid to rest as Willoughby Wells recalled,

> On the morning of the eighteenth day of the siege, three horsemen, of the advanced Guard, came in sight. I watched them intently as they approached us, and when they were a mile and a half away, I knew we had spent our last night in that camp—that relief was at hand and our long watch and vigilance was over. One of those three was one of the soldiers who had left us eighteen [fifteen] nights before. . . . The first man to greet us was the man whose horse gave out.[9]

After more than nine days on the march, during which fourteen horses of the Sixth Iowa were lost to an early morning Indian raid, Colonel Dill's rescue party finally reached the emigrant corral. Fisk tried to persuade the colonel to provide more troops to escort the wagon train as far as the Yellowstone. But Dill refused, citing that he was under orders only to escort the train back to the fort. Fearing his expedition was about to come to a dreadful end, Fisk desperately pleaded with the emigrants to continue on without an escort. A few were persuaded at first, but the next morning, all were ready to follow the military relief back. "[The] Captain very reluctantly turned back," Wells remembered, "but as the whole train left, he fell in and followed."

Dill's relief detail and the Fisk wagon train arrived back at Fort Rice on the thirtieth without incident. A small number of the emigrants remained at the fort for the winter hoping to finish the crossing in the spring. But most of them returned to Iowa or Minnesota, never making a second attempt to seek wealth in Montana.

Fanny Kelly, who had been with Sitting Bull's people at Killdeer Mountain and who Captain Fisk was unable to rescue, was at least fortunate to have been held by a band of Sioux with which the compassionate Sitting Bull carried influence. Realizing that holding a white woman captive would not improve their relations with the government, the Hunkpapa released Kelly at Fort Sully in December of that year. In 1873, the story of her experience was published in a book entitled *Narrative of My Captivity Among the Sioux Indians,* which became widely popular.

Captain Fisk vigorously defended his actions of not following the order to use the northern route and then leaving Sully's trail at the Cannonball River. The military criticized his behavior but in the end took no action against him. After the news of the poisoned hardtack incident reached the public, Fisk and the military were bitterly condemned in some eastern newspapers. But in the West the action received wide approval, reflecting the attitude of the public after the Dakota War.

James Fisk was mustered out of service in June 1865. Despite the failure of the 1864 expedition, he still remained a viable leader for overland migration. In 1866 he led another expedition of about 160 wagons and more than three hundred people to the Montana goldfields. Following the northern trail of his first two expeditions, Fisk may have been more strongly convinced by the government to use the established route again. Certainly his memory of the deaths of soldiers and civilians when he tried to blaze his own trail would remain with him. As for the one-time gold seekers and settlers who followed the bold captain in 1864, a part of them would remain on the open prairie within the sod walls of what became known to history as Fort Dilts.

# The Notorious John L. Campbell

IN 1862 when Eugene Marshall described the Fifth Iowa Cavalry as having been branded a regiment of "horse thieves and jayhawkers," the behavior of some of the companies as units and several individuals in the regiment certainly contributed to that reputation. Among them was a Minnesota volunteer, John L. Campbell, who may have played a large role in developing that stigma. Campbell was a member of Captain von Minden's "German company," Company G of the Fifth Iowa, later Company A of Brackett's Battalion. At the age of twenty-seven, Campbell mustered in with the First Company of Minnesota Cavalry on September 30, 1861, as one of its original volunteers. At the time of his enlistment he had already developed a reputation of being a man of questionable behavior.

Jack, as he was known by most, was the youngest son of mixed-blood parents. His father, Scott, a mixed-blood Dakota who died in 1850, was for several years a French and Dakota interpreter at Fort Snelling. His mother, Margaret, was a mixed-blood Menominee and Dakota Indian. Jack was a trapper and fur trader before the war. It was during this time, after his father's death, that he began to lead an infamous and abandoned life. It was believed he had committed, or was involved in, several murders while a young man.

Campbell was a strikingly handsome man, described by one historian as, "a man of more than usual physical beauty [who] had long curly, black hair, dark, expressive eyes, and a finely proportioned figure." He was also a deceptively persuasive man. Jack had the ability to talk his way into or out of most situations. And when his arguments failed to liberate him from a predicament, he usually found a way to minimize the outcome. He was also a man who pursued adventure whenever the opportunity presented itself.

While serving with the Fifth Iowa, Campbell's reputation for cunning and adventure attracted the attention of his commanders. He was recruited as a scout and became known as one of the most valuable scouts in the army, along with George Northrup. Like Northrup, Jack pressed his spirit of adventure to its limits.

After the Tullahoma campaign he joined the Confederate army in order to spy on General Bragg's strength in Chattanooga. Campbell collected a wealth of information about the Confederates there, detailing on paper gun emplacements and calibers, troop strength, their arms, and the names of commanders. Deserting his rebel unit, he made a dangerous trek back to Union lines and reported personally to General Rosecrans with the information. The general highly commended Campbell for his actions.

It was Campbell's value as a scout that allowed him to build on his notorious reputation. He was often absent from the Fifth Iowa for days and sometimes weeks as he was allowed to come and go as he pleased. It was that freedom that gave Campbell opportunities to continue his lawless behavior. Colonel Lowe once stated that Campbell "never accumulated anything honestly." Lowe also reported that Campbell had been identified by citizens for being "engaged in a series of highway robberies." In his diary, Eugene Marshall described Jack as being "noted for daring and rascality, passing a large part of his time in the guardhouse under charges of various kinds. Once or twice he was court-martialed."

In March 1863, Campbell was accused of robbing a man by the name of William Ventress in Dickson County, Tennessee. With the aid of the man's slaves, Campbell stole three wagons and teams with food supplies and several thousand dollars in Tennessee money, which was dug out of the floor of Ventress's smokehouse. Campbell managed to avoid conviction for the robbery by escaping from the guardhouse during his court martial. Instead he was fined six months' pay for being absent without leave.

Known also for his womanizing, Campbell pursued an affair with a Mrs. Underwood. It was common knowledge among the men in his company that the two had killed the woman's husband with poison. When the Fifth Iowa Cavalry was re-enlisted and sent home on veterans furlough, Campbell first headed south to the home of his mistress and robbed her before departing for Minnesota.

It was during the first year of service in the South that the mystery of Jack Campbell began to develop. In the summer of 1862, Campbell spoke to others in his company about the plight of the Dakota in Minnesota. He appeared to be well informed about Indian matters there. So much so that he made predictions about a war that would take place that summer. Confiding in his friends, Campbell named a date the fighting would begin, where attacks would be made, and who the leaders would be.

Campbell's predictions were not taken seriously until later that year when news of the Dakota war in Minnesota reached the troops of the Fifth Iowa. It seems his predictions proved to be accurate and that the fighting had begun only about two weeks later than what he foretold. Curiously, Campbell was absent from the regiment without orders during the entire course of the Dakota War, returning later that winter. But as usual he managed to dodge any serious penalties against him for his disappearance.

Most of Jack's family lived at the Lower Sioux Agency on the Minnesota River. Raised as Christians with a lifestyle like that of the whites, most of Jack's siblings, including his mother, wanted no part in the war. His mother and his brother Antoine and his family were forced to live with the war party.

During the conflict, Antoine protected the captured whites who were mostly women and children. After the decisive battle at Wood Lake, he convinced Little Crow, who led the attacks, to release the captives unharmed, bringing an end to the conflict. Later, Antoine was a witness against some of the Indian prisoners who stood trial for their actions. He was not charged himself for having any complicity in the fighting. The next year, Antoine was a scout for General Sibley during his expedition into Dakota Territory.

Two other brothers of Jack Campbell, Hypolite and Baptiste, also were unwilling participants in the beginning. Both took action to protect peaceful Dakotas, whites, and the Campbell family from being harmed by the war parties. But the fever of the war caught up with them, and both men were implicated as willing participants. Hypolite escaped capture and fled to Manitoba. Baptiste was captured, tried, convicted for his crimes, and executed on December 26, 1862, with thirty-seven others in a mass public hanging at Mankato.

When Jack returned to his regiment that winter, he made no secret about his anger at the Dakota defeat and his brother's execution. In his diary Eugene Marshall wrote, "he has often been heard to say that he would have revenge upon Mankato for the hanging of his brother."

After the three Minnesota companies of cavalry returned home on furlough in February 1864, Campbell, arriving a month later, as usual was frequently absent from duty. He was assigned to the detail that would receive the new Canadian ponies at La Crosse, but again Campbell was missing. During that time, two infantrymen, half-blood Ojibwe, were found dead near the town of Mendota across the river from Fort Snelling. One of the men lived long enough to name Jack Campbell as the man who poisoned them.

Campbell was soon found and placed in the guardhouse at the fort. After the newly formed Brackett's Battalion left the fort for Dakota Territory, Campbell escaped from the guardhouse in the company of a former Confederate soldier. Far removed from events at home, Major Brackett continued to list Campbell as being, "In arrest at Ft. Snelling," unaware he was now listed by the army as a deserter.

During the remainder of 1864 and the early part of 1865, the whereabouts and activities of Jack Campbell are generally unknown. The last sighting of Campbell and his cellmate was between Shakopee and Belle Plaine, Minnesota, where they stole a couple of horses. It was believed by some that Jack made his way north to British territory where he contacted his brother Hypolite. While he was there, he rounded up about a hundred Dakota fugitives who had fled Minnesota. Split up into small bands, Campbell's renegades filtered back into the state with a plan to attack and destroy the city of Mankato.

On August 11, 1864, several sightings of these renegades were made near Mankato. One farmer and his son were shot at and wounded by one band of hostiles, and another farmer was killed by renegades on the same day. Several other attacks, without bloodshed, and more sightings were made in the area.

Military detachments and militia groups were dispatched to hunt down the marauders, including one company of the Second Minnesota Cavalry and twenty men of Brackett's Battalion who were on detached service at Fort Snelling. After an exhaustive search, none of the renegades were found or captured. It was later speculated that Campbell may have been involved in the attacks. But that notion is unlikely due to the fact that he escaped from Fort Snelling on the same day as the attacks.

If Campbell was leading a returning band to make attacks, two things would be needed for the venture—food and weapons. Jack had a uncanny ability for gaining information and knowing where to find what he wanted. Marshall T. Fall from Garden City, Minnesota, a lieutenant in Company B of Brackett's Battalion, was in the habit of sending part of his pay to Andrew Jewett, a relative in Garden City, for safe keeping. Lieutenant Fall was expecting to win a bid for a farm south of Mankato. He had sent five hundred dollars to Jewett, who would hold the money and make the payment for the land, which would occur in the spring of 1865.

Jewett had been a prominent citizen of Garden City where for a time he was postmaster and was active in county politics. In 1864 he had purchased some property about five miles west of Garden City near the settlement of Rapidan on which he built a log house. Occupying the new home were Andrew, his wife Harriet, their two-year-old son William, and Andrew's parents, Mark and Susan Jewett. The next year Andrew was elected town justice during Rapidan's first town meeting.

In the early morning of May 2, 1865, a Mr. Harlow, a neighbor of the Jewetts, arrived at the Jewetts' home to borrow a wagon. He had heard the sound of gunfire from the direction of the Jewett place about two hours earlier but thought nothing of it. As he approached the Jewett cabin, he discovered a most grisly scene. Harriet Jewett was lying dead in the path with a gunshot wound near the heart. A few feet way he found young William unconscious with a severe blow to the head but alive. Closer to the house Harlow came upon Andrew Jewett also dead with a bullet wound to the chest and a deadly blow to the head from what appeared to be a tomahawk.

In a state of shock, Harlow entered the cabin to search for Andrew's parents. Inside he found more horror. The elder Mr. Jewett was lying on the floor in a pool of blood near the dining table where it appeared the family was seated for their morning breakfast when the attack came. He had been struck on the head, leaving an open gash in his skull, but was also still alive. The elder Mrs. Jewett was an invalid and confined to bed. It was there she was found, covered in blood, with her head and face smashed beyond recognition.

The news of the Jewett murders soon reached the citizens of Rapidan and Garden City where men were organized to comb the area in search of the culprits. Back at the Jewett property, Charles Tyler, a hired hand and relative of the Jewetts, was found dead from a gunshot wound and an arrow in his chest, twenty rods north of the house where he was chopping wood.

The dead and wounded were brought to Garden City where Mark Jewett, for a short time the next morning, regained consciousness. Barely able to speak, the elder Jewett told of five or six Indians bursting into the house with guns and bows. It was the only information he could provide before he died later that day. Two-year-old William Jewett was to be the only survivor of the attack.

On the day of the murders a Mr. O. W. Dodge, who was riding on a road from Mankato spreading the news of the horrible tragedy, came upon a mixed-blood Indian walking toward town dressed in civilian clothes. Dodge stopped the stranger, who suspiciously tried to avoid him, and began questioning the man. The man's answers seemed evasive, which further aroused Dodge's suspicions. Dodge drew his revolver and arrested him.

The stranger was brought to Mankato where by now the entire population was informed of the Jewett murders. A crowd gathered at the house where the long-black-haired man was being held. More questions were addressed to the man who claimed his name was Pelky and gave an account of himself of having nothing to do with the murders. The man's explanations began to convince his captors until a Mr. Isaac Marks appeared who knew the man well. Marks identified the man as John Campbell, declaring he had a particularly bad reputation. Campbell was placed in the county jail while people began to investigate his explanations, soon learning that Campbell's stories were contradictory or false.

In the evening a group of citizens dragged Campbell out of the Mankato jail, placed a rope around his neck, and tried to pry a confession from him while tightening up the rope. But it was to no avail. The prisoner was searched and his clothing inspected for clues. He was found to be wearing two pair of ladies white wool stockings, a pair of ill-fitting men's shoes, a broadcloth coat, and a new pair of pants. The clothing was taken from him, wrapped into a bundle, and carried to Garden City to be inspected by relatives and friends of the Jewett family.

The bundle was first brought to the home of Eva Tyler, sister of the young man who was murdered with the Jewetts. Eva had recently worked for the Jewetts and was familiar with their clothing. She perfectly described the coat of Mark Jewett, including a small repair on the sleeve, before seeing what was brought to her. When the coat from Campbell was shown to her, she identified it immediately as Mark Jewett's. The pants she also recognized as a pair owned by the elder Jewett. She declared that the stockings looked like ones belonging to the elder Mrs. Jewett and the shoes like a pair of Andrew's. The clothing was also positively identified by others in Garden City as possessions of the Jewett family. One pair of stockings were recognized by one woman as having been knitted by grandmother Jewett.

The clothing was taken back to Mankato with the news of who the real owners were. During the night while the clothing was inspected at Garden City, a Mr. Peter Kelley, who had no knowledge of the murders, arrived in Mankato. Kelley brought news of what he had heard from Scott Campbell, Jr., a brother of John Campbell. Scott had been visited by his brother and learned that Jack was leading a band of marauders with the intent of attacking Mankato. Kelley knew the Campbell family and was at once taken to the jail where he immediately identified Jack.

By morning, realizing the evidence was against him, Campbell began to change his story. He admitted he was John Campbell and was a deserter from Brackett's Battalion but claimed he was taken prisoner by a large band of Indians and forced to travel with them. He said they took his own clothes from him and forced him to wear the Jewetts' clothing without knowledge of who the clothing belonged to or how the items were acquired. He managed to escape from the band on the same day he was picked up by Dodge. But Campbell's story was unconvincing. It became clear to everyone that Campbell was one of the murderers.

The news of the Jewett murders and Campbell's capture quickly spread. The morning afterward, people from all over the county, nearly a thousand strong, began to pour into Mankato and surround the jail. Speeches were made on street corners. Some favored an immediate hanging, others pleaded for due process of the law. Soon it became apparent that the general attitude of the crowd was for a lynching as people shouted, "hang the villain." Many believed General Sibley and his troops could arrive on the scene at any moment and carry the prisoner off for a military trial that could result in an unsatisfactory verdict.

As a compromise, it was decided to hold a jury trial in the street by the citizens. A judge, prosecuting attorney, defense attorney, and a twelve-man jury were selected. Campbell pleaded not guilty and told an even more elaborate story of his capture, of how he was forced to wear the Jewetts' clothing, and of his escape. The prosecuting attorney pointed out the clothing evidence and Campbell's conflicting stories. After two hours of trial, the jury retired to deliberate. A half an hour later, the jury returned with a verdict of guilty and a recommendation that Campbell should be held for the district court.

For the next several minutes the crowd turned into a near riot. A majority of them demanded that Campbell be hanged immediately. A large minority, including the town's sheriff, tried to enforce the jury's recommendation and began escorting the prisoner back to the jail. But the hanging party tried to stop the others as Campbell was being pushed and pulled in two directions. Soon guns and knives were drawn by the lynch party. Realizing the struggle was about to turn to bloodshed, the jury enforcement crowd withdrew.

A rope was fastened to an appropriate limb of a nearby basswood tree. Campbell was placed on a wagon under the limb and the noose placed around his neck. The wagon was pulled from under him, but in the hangmen's haste, they neglected to tie Campbell's hands. Jack reached up and grabbed the rope above him and then began yelling for a priest.

The lynch party granted the request, bringing the wagon back under the condemned man. Father Sommereisen pushed his way through the crowd and boarded the wagon. After consoling Campbell with prayer, the two conversed in French, presumably for a confession. Campbell's hands were then secured after time had expired. When the wagon was again pulled away, Campbell clung to it for a few feet, then slid off, swinging back several feet. After about twenty minutes, John Campbell was pronounced dead.

Apparently Campbell had told Father Sommereisen where to find a bundle of money that he had hidden in the bedding of his bunk at the jail. A quick search of the bunk produced a bundle of about $470.00, believed to be that of Lieutenant Fall who had sent the cash to Andrew Jewett.

For two weeks after the Jewett murders, volunteers combed the countryside for the rest of Campbell's party. Posses were organized at Garden City and Rapidan. Militias from South Bend, Vernon, Sterling, and Mapleton picketed roads between towns. On one day, a detachment of cavalry from Mankato tracked and found five Indians on the banks of a river where a short skirmish took place, resulting in the death of one of the troopers. The renegades escaped.

Apparently the small band that accompanied Campbell was reluctant to leave the area. Their camps were found in several locations, and other encounters occurred as they attempted to steal horses from farms. One ten-year-old boy, Frank York, was shot and killed by them in an ambush. Later another man was wounded while preventing them from stealing a horse. Finally the band managed to slip out of the state into Dakota Territory.

It was there that friendly Indians, employed by the army as scouts, finally ended the raiders' flight. The scouts were stationed at various picket posts between the Sheyenne River and the James River for the protection of Minnesota's western border. In the middle of May, four of the scouts ambushed five Indians who were slowly making their way across the prairie on horseback. Three of the raiding party were shot and killed. A fourth man was wounded and captured. The fifth was wounded but managed to escape. Two horses belonging to the Jewetts were recovered from this party as well as more of the Jewetts' clothing and silverware bearing their initials.

In the end, five of the six men who attacked the Jewett home were brought to their demise, bringing to an end three years of recurrent attacks by such renegades in southern Minnesota after the Dakota war. Even though John Campbell was not proven guilty for the Jewett murders in a legal trial, there is little doubt among historians that he was directly involved in the attack and most likely planned it and led it. His execution was the last of its kind in connection with the conflict.

# Extended Service:
# The Expedition of 1865

AT THE CLOSE of the 1864 Northwestern Indian Expedition, General Sully's two brigades returned to their home districts for new assignments. The Second Brigade departed for Minnesota where the Second Minnesota Cavalry was split up by companies to garrison various forts and outposts along Minnesota's western frontier. Captain Jones's Third Minnesota Battery was also divided and sent to some of the same posts. The Eighth Minnesota turned in their mounts at Fort Snelling and immediately embarked for Tennessee. Arriving at Murfreesboro the regiment was soon engaged in heavy fighting and hard campaigning against the Confederates. At the war's end, the tattered Eighth was in camp at Charlotte, North Carolina.

The First Brigade with General Sully, as well as several settlers from the Fisk wagon train, returned to Sioux City, arriving on October 20. The Sixth Iowa Cavalry and the detachment of the Seventh Iowa were also detailed to garrison posts along the Missouri River and elsewhere for the winter. Major Brackett seemed certain this Minnesota battalion would be staying at or near Sioux City. He was unaware that Sully had promised General Sibley that Brackett's Battalion would return to Minnesota after the expedition was completed. Upon the brigade's arrival at Sioux City, Sibley reminded Sully of the commitment. Brackett's Battalion was then ordered to winter quarters at Fort Ridgely, Minnesota.

Lieutenant Joseph Porter of Company D, with a detachment of forty men from his company, would be left behind to provide an additional garrison on the Dakota prairie. On November 11, the detachment arrived at a lonely outpost named Camp Edwards in eastern Dakota Territory, a few miles from the Minnesota border. The camp consisted of a single log hut surrounded by five-foot-high earthen breastworks. It had been occupied by troops only once before more than six years earlier and then for only one month. With winter fast approaching, the men could waste no time in refurbishing the remnants of what would be their winter quarters.

On October 31, Brackett's Battalion left Sioux City for Fort Ridgely. Because the prairie was nearly barren from two years of drought, grain depots were set up along the route to supply the battalion's horses and wagon teams with adequate feed during the march. About fifteen miles south of the fort, thirty more men from Company D were left at the stockade at Leavenworth for a winter garrison. Arriving at Fort Ridgely on November 9 with the bulk of the battalion, Sergeant Major Eugene Marshall recorded that from the time the battalion left Fort Snelling on May 2 they had marched more than 2,100 miles.

At Fort Ridgely, site of two fierce battles against the Dakota during the 1862 war, the battalion was encamped with a variety of other troops for the winter. Along with Brackett's men, the garrison included three companies of the Second Minnesota Cavalry, one company of the First Connecticut Cavalry, a section of the Third Minnesota Battery, and one company of the First United States Volunteers. The latter were former Confederate prisoners, mostly deserters, who volunteered for duty with the Federal army on the northern frontier and were known as "Whitewashed Rebs" to the army or, among themselves, "Galvanized Yankees."

After completing a hard campaign in Dakota Territory, Brackett's men expected the army to be prepared for their arrival at Fort Ridgely, providing for them reasonably comfortable quarters. Instead they found the fort was ill prepared for such a large garrison. "The quarters were built for four companies," Marshall noted in his diary, "but four full companies crowd them to their utmost capacities. Company C occupies one set of quarters & is terribly crowded far too much for comfort or health." There was only enough stable room for a portion of the horses and mules as well. As winter approached the men found themselves hauling logs eight or nine miles to a sawmill in the river valley to make lumber for more stables, which they would construct themselves.

As Brackett's Battalion settled into its winter quarters, a few changes were made with the officers of two of the companies. Company A would now have a completely new set of officers. In early November, Captain von Minden was promoted to major and transferred to the six companies of the Independent Battalion of Minnesota Cavalry, formerly commanded by Major Edwin A. C. Hatch, who resigned in June due to illness. Von Minden would now be second in command to Hatch's replacement, Lieutenant Colonel C. Powell Adams.

The new captain of von Minden's German company was Albert T. Phelps. Originally a private in the company, Phelps had recently been its first sergeant. Also, First Lieutenant August Matthaus and Second Lieutenant Joseph Buck were discharged in December. They were replaced by Alfred H. Foote and Adam Lindig, both of whom had risen up through the ranks in the company from the rank of private.

It was the change in Company C that would create a great deal of concern in Brackett's Battalion after January 1865. Captain Shelley had not reenlisted and was discharged on January 31. In the natural order of promotion, Lieutenant Neely was in line to succeed Shelley. But due to Neely's drunken behavior over the course of the last three years, particularly in 1864, the men, not only in his company but throughout the battalion, were determined to prevent his promotion.

In the early summer of 1864, during one of his famous drunken episodes, Neely had a particularly bad run-in with Major Brackett. As a result, Neely was placed under arrest and court martialed but got by with a light sentence. Brackett sent his report of the incident to General Pope in Milwaukee. Soon after, Brackett received a letter from Pope in which the general expressed great reservations about the mild sentence: "It is not fitting and proper that a person found guilty of such offenses should hold a commission in the service of the United States." But Pope reluctantly approved the action stating, "Lieutenant Mortimer Neely, Company C, Brackett's Battalion Minnesota Volunteers, will be released from arrest and will return to his duty."

After Captain Shelley was discharged, Brackett, always lighthearted, indicated he would allow Neely's promotion. But Brackett's officers vowed to block the promotion. A petition, sent to Minnesota's adjutant general, was drafted and signed by most of the officers and many of the enlisted men in the battalion. The letter listed several of Neely's past escapades accompanied by a plea to prevent his promotion. But the military in its usual fashion turned a blind eye to the men in the field. In the early part of April, a frustrated Eugene Marshall entered in his diary,

> The men of Company "C" met a rebuff tonight in as much as they rec'd from the Adjutant General's Office a letter to the effect that

Lieut. Neely must be commissioned captain Co. "C" upon the recommendations rec'd, the recommendations being from Gen. Sibley and Major Brackett and the letter being over the signature of
Gov. Miller.[1]

On April 12, Neely was promoted to captain.

Brackett's Battalion whiled away the winter on monotonous garrison duty, involving "drill and discipline." Also keeping the troop's
minds occupied was news from the war in the South and speculation
on what their orders would be in the spring. The men had every reason to believe that the Union army was making great strides against
the Confederates and that the war would be winding down soon. They
were more eager to take part in a Union victory than to spend another
season on the barren plains.

In March, Major Brackett spent the month in St. Paul serving on
a board of courts marshal, hearing several cases against soldiers for a
variety of offenses. While there, Brackett held meetings with General
Sibley about what the prospects would be concerning the battalion's
duties that year. Proving to be the most reliable of the officers, Captain
Barton was left in command of the battalion during Brackett's absence.
But it was Sergeant Major Marshall with whom Brackett often com-
municated. At the end of the month Brackett sent a letter to Marshall,
informing him,

> Sully wrote to Gen'l Sibley that I would be ordered out with him.
> Gen'l said it was intended that the Battalion would go south, as he
> has just rec'd orders from the war dep't to forward all veterans to
> the front, he still thinks we will go south.[2]

Later in the letter he reminded Marshall to " . . . keep an eye on
those you think intend to play sick."

General Pope in Milwaukee now believed that the government's
policy of making treaties and extending annuities to the plains Indians had been a giant failure. He tried to convince President Lincoln
that "the Indian problem" should be placed solely in the hands of the
military. Raw military power, Pope reasoned, would force the hostile
parties to sue for peace. But Lincoln was too preoccupied with the war
in the South to change policy now. Pope believed he had no other choice
but to plan another expedition against the Sioux on the northern plains.

Pope granted General Sully's request to retain Brackett's Battalion for another campaign into Dakota Territory.

The battalion was to again join General Sully at Sioux City, Iowa, to complete the formation of a single brigade for the new expedition. In early April, a late winter snowstorm socked in the garrison at Fort Ridgely, delaying the battalion's departure. After Company D's Leavenworth garrison arrived, Brackett's Battalion was finally able to march out of the fort on the morning of April 8. Due to a lack of horses and weapons, several of the men marched out dismounted, and many were yet without arms.

The next day the battalion arrived at St. Peter where they expected to be supplied with horses, weapons, and supplies for the campaign. The remainder of Company D, Lieutenant Porter's detachment from Camp Edwards, joined the battalion there after spending a dreary, cold winter on the open plains. Major Brackett met the troops there on the tenth, arriving by steamboat on the Minnesota River from St. Paul.

On the twelfth, the news that the men had long waited for finally arrived. Marshall wrote, "Glorious news came to us this morning. Lee has surrendered his whole army." On the ninth, General Robert E. Lee surrendered his Confederate army to General Ulysses S. Grant at Appomattox, Virginia. With little fighting left, the war was drawing to a close. "Well, the celebration went off without much trouble," Marshall wrote. "The men did not get very drunk and the little cannon was fired one hundred and fifty times without accident."

The men were enlisted for a three-year term of service or until the end of the war, whichever came first. The war in the South was not completely over yet, and so the men continued to go through the motions of preparing for the Dakota expedition, believing the end was near and they would be sent home. However, the army was not able to replace the volunteers in the field with regular troops anytime soon, and the expedition into Dakota Territory was to deal with an Indian problem, not a Confederate one.

A few days later, the men's rising spirits from the news of the war's end suddenly collapsed. The unthinkable news of President Lincoln's assassination reached St. Peter. Marshall's diary entry read,

> The people all feel very sad over the death of Lincoln. No event within the range of possibility could have shocked the sense of a na-

tion as this has done. They feel that a great man has fallen, & general belief is that history will assign him a place second to none but George Washington as a patriot, a statesman, and a just man.[3]

After receiving the additional horses and weapons and thirty wagons loaded with supplies for Sully's brigade pulled by 180 mules, Brackett's Battalion marched out of St. Peter on April 17 under a heavy rain. Through frequent rains and muddy roads the battalion reached Fairmont, Minnesota. There they were brought to the realization that not everyone in the North was saddened by Lincoln's death. A few days earlier one man in town was hanged in a tree after expressing his joy over the news of the assassination. After the battalion's arrival, one of the troopers had made plans to accompany a young lady to a dance in town. But later he told her to stay home when she informed him that she was going to the dance to celebrate Lincoln's death.

Continuing their march south, the battalion was bogged down again on the Iowa border by another late-season snowstorm. Five horses and two mules perished in the blizzard. On April 30 they passed through Sioux City, making camp on the banks of the Big Sioux River on the Dakota border.

At Sioux City the battalion was reunited with their comrades of the First Brigade from the 1864 expedition. The same elements of the Sixth and Seventh Iowa Cavalry, Pope's Battery, and only Company B of the Dakota Cavalry, along with Brackett's Battalion would conduct the expedition without the company of a second brigade. Sully again was under orders to march to the mouth of the Powder River and to establish a new military post there. And again, it appeared that another slow moving emigrant wagon train was waiting to follow.

More good news from the South was pouring in at Sioux City. Significant Confederate surrenders were being made in a short period of time, which gave the men every reason to believe they would not commence with the expedition. Anticipation of being mustered out of service in a matter of days ran high. "The men are in a feverish state of anxiety as regards [to] their discharge," Marshall wrote. But like the news of Lincoln's assassination, which brought the men into mournful despair, news of their own future again dashed their hopes. They were informed that only veteran troops would be held in service until the regular army could take over. This "damnable act of injustice" infuriated the troops at Sioux City. But, surprisingly, no major eruptions occurred.

Sully's expedition was delayed at Sioux City while the army contemplated the status of volunteer troops. His orders for the campaign also changed. Instead of marching to the Powder River with a civilian wagon train, the expedition would march north along the east side of the Missouri to engage possible hostiles if need be, but mostly to establish peaceful relations with the Sioux, make treaties, and develop an understanding between the Indians and the government.

During the month of May, Major Brackett kept his battalion busy with drill in an attempt to take their minds off the fact that they would not be discharged soon. With heightened anticipation of their release, the mood of the troops changed frequently, from threats of mass desertion to subdued acceptance of remaining in service for another expedition. Captain Neely also used the idle time to renew his disruptive behavior.

After several more drunken episodes, Neely again was placed under arrest by Major Brackett. But Brackett was still willing to give Neely another chance to redeem himself. Brackett had Sergeant Major Marshall draw up a confession and pledge of sobriety, which was signed by Neely. On the evening of May 19, while Company C was in formation for roll call with Captain Neely facing his men, the orderly sergeant read the draft to the company, which in part stated,

> I acknowledge to you that I behaved in a manner which was disgraceful to me as an officer and a soldier and which was subversive of good discipline in the army and an example which no enlisted man should copy. . . . I have taken a solemn oath in the presence of Almighty God that so long as I remain captain of this company I will not drink another drop of intoxicating liquor on any pretext whatever.[4]

In his diary Marshall wrote, "When it was read, men looked at each other in silent wonder & tonight have hardly found their tongues."

At the end of June a paper was passed among the officers of the battalion for their signatures to indicate a voluntary intent to remain in the military after being mustered out of volunteer service. Captain Neely was the only man to sign the paper. Marshall wrote, "I pity the army if it is to be officered by such men as he is." But as usual, Neely's

alcoholism was too overpowering. On several occasions in the following months, he was found in a drunken stupor. Once in July when his
company was prepared to take up the march, Neely was too drunk to
take command. On August 31, after getting more than his share of
chances, Neely was placed under arrest by Major Brackett for the last
time. Captain Neely was relieved from command on September 3 and
ordered to Sioux City until the battalion returned. Company D's Lieutenant Porter was then placed in command of Company C.

In June, Sully's brigade collected again at Fort Sully to make final
preparations for the march. Detached from Minnesota's Independent
Battalion, Major von Minden rejoined the expedition, serving on the
general's staff as acting inspector general. On July 5, the Northwestern Indian Expedition began its march north toward Fort Rice.

The 1865 campaign was conducted with little difficulty and was
generally uneventful. Improved weather brought the prairie grasses
back, which made the march for the horses and wagon teams less stress-
ful. But still, on occasion, the troops had to dig wells for fresh water at
a few campsites.

On July 13, the expedition made camp opposite Fort Rice where six
companies of "galvanized Yankees" had spent a miserable winter. Ten
percent of them had died from various diseases. At the fort, General
Sully conducted negotiations with the leaders of various Sioux bands,
many of whom were involved in the fighting against Sully at Killdeer
Mountain and in the Badlands during the previous year. For several
days Indians arrived from all directions to sign treaties.

Resuming the march on the twenty-third, Sully's command headed
northeast for Devils Lake expecting to encounter unfriendly Sioux
camped there but found none.

Nineteen-year-old Corporal Charles A. Bennett, who began his service with the First Minnesota Mounted Rangers in 1862 and was now
in his second year with Company D of Brackett's Battalion, had been
keeping daily entries in his diary since leaving the stockade at Leavenworth, Minnesota. Much of what was seen and experienced by the
common cavalryman in the battalion during the 1865 expedition was
recorded by Bennett:

Sat. [July] 22nd
    Went over to the Fort today and bought a wagon. Sixteen of us
    went in and Bought it. We paid ten dollars a piece. We got orders

to march tomorrow. A man in Company M of the 6th Iowa Cavalry committed sueside by shooting himself in the Right Breast with a Revolver. He expired. . . .

### Tues. 25th Camp 25

I was out a hunting today. I got into a large herd of Buffalo and had a great deal of fun. Can't say I killed any because there was so many firing that it was impossible to tell Whitch killed them. There was quite a number killed.

### Thurs. 27th

. . . there was thousands of buffalo on our flanks today. The Boys had a great time killing them.

### Sat. 29th

We arrived at Devils Lake. The water in this Lake not very good. Marched 20 miles.

### Tuesday, August 1st

Maj. VonMinden went out to examine the Lake today. Fifteen of us went with him. We found an outlet to [the] Lake. This was not known of before. It rained in the forenoon.

### Wed. 2nd

Broke camp this morning and took up our line of march for Mouse River. . . . It rained.

### Thurs. 3rd

. . . it was good water four miles from Mouse River, there was timber, there was hundreds of Buffalo all around Camp. It rained.

### Friday 4th

Camped on Mouse River. This River is clear running water and very good, plenty of fish.

### Sunday 6th

Camped on a small Lake. There was lots of Buffalo. There was 4 men went out of each Company to hunt. After we got into camp the Lake was full of young geese and ducks. The Boys caught some two hundred of them.

### Mon. 7th

. . . made a long march of 33 miles. Camped on a creek. There was several hundred Buffalo on our right and left.

Tues. 8th
Camp on Creek . . . about 4 miles from Fort Berthold.

Sun. 13th
There was quite a discovery made here today. There was a burning volcano discovered. They dug down some six or eight feet and found fire.

Monday 14th
. . . discovered a hot Spring.

Thurs. 17th
Our company was on Pickett today. There was some hostile Indians seen. . . . I am on Stable Guard tonight.

Sat. 19th
Last night just after dark there was one of the worst storms that I ever saw. It rained and hailed for about fifteen minutes and in that length of time it fell to the depth of about ten inches. . . . There is a small creek in front of our camp and in ten minutes after it had quit raining it had raised about ten feet.

Fri. 25th
We have made a very long march today. It was very warm and we suffered for water. We marched until sundown and arrived at Ft. Rice. Marched 37½ miles. I received one Letter from Leavenworth and one from Chatfield.

Sunday 27th
A corporal in Company C went out this morning and has [not] returned. They have searched for him but to no avail.

Monday 28th
Corporal Jameson was found this morning about one quarter of a mile from camp. . . . he was shot by Indians. There was three Indians seen near that spot yesterday on Picket.

Tues. 29th
I went over to the Fort. They caught all three Indians today that they think killed Jameson.

Tues. [September] 5th
Broke camp early this morning and took up our line of march for Fort Sully.

Wed. 13th
Marched 22 miles, camped on the Missouri River below Fort Sully.
Our Company was on Advance Guard.[5]

Finding no Indians to engage at Devils Lake, the expedition turned
northwest to the Mouse River, then south to Fort Berthold on the Missouri, arriving there on August 8. Near the camps, natural wonders of
the earth attracted the soldiers' attention. Marshall elaborated in his
diary what Corporal Bennett described as a volcano discovery:

> There has been a discovery of a coal bed near our camp which is on
> fire and appears to have been so for a long time. . . . All that was
> thrown out was coke and cinders. . . . The coke thrown out took fire
> and made a bright hot blaze in the open air. . . . A space of several
> acres appears to have been burnt over. . . . I think coal is abundant
> in this country.[6]

At the fort General Sully negotiated with Medicine Bear, chief of
the Yanktonai Sioux. Medicine Bear told of his involvement in both
fights with Sully the previous year and described having been wounded.
He also claimed to have lost several hundred warriors against Sully in
two years of fighting. Medicine Bear wanted peace but told Sully he
would not make an agreement with him. He preferred to come to terms
with some other general or government official.

Sully also visited with the Ree Indians who complained of dry
weather and asked the general if he would pray for rain. Later, the Ree
leaders may have thought that the General went too far with his
prayers. On the evening of August 18, Eugene Marshall recorded in
his diary the event Corporal Bennett had also noted: "And tonight there
has been a most fearful shower with wind, rain & hail, to say nothing
of thunder & lightning. Our camp was flooded, horses were stampeded,
and we had a fearful time for an hour or so."[7] Some of the companies
in the expedition lost all of their tents and most of their equipment and
spare clothing in the flash flood. The headquarters camp was also hit
hard.

Deciding against marching farther west above the Missouri in pursuit of the Sioux, Sully turned south toward Fort Rice to conclude the
expedition. Upon Sully's arrival, it was learned that the fort had been
under attack by hostiles who had been repulsed by the garrison. When

the Sioux warriors learned of Sully's approach, they left the area. But the threat had not completely passed.

A day after making camp opposite the fort, Corporal Horace Jameson of Brackett's Company C failed to return from being out cutting tent poles for the camp. After an extensive search, Jameson's body was found with a gunshot and arrow wound in a thicket about three hundred yards from camp. Jameson, a thirty-two-old farmer who had been with his company from the beginning and was one of the battalion's eight wounded at Killdeer Mountain, left a wife and two children. The men of Brackett's Battalion were so angered by his death that they threatened to "kill all the Indians they meet."

By September 13, Brackett's Battalion was encamped near Fort Sully fully expecting to receive their discharge orders. Most of the other elements of the expedition were now being mustered out of service. Portions of the Sixth Iowa Cavalry had already received discharge notices while the brigade was in camp near Fort Berthold. But there was no word yet for Brackett's Battalion.

The men were becoming more confused and gradually outraged by the prospects for their future when the battalion was being split up and sent to various posts along the Missouri River and elsewhere in southern Dakota Territory. Company C was posted at Fort Randall. By mid-October, Company D was near the Minnesota border on the Big Sioux River at Sioux Falls. The other companies were divided up among other posts scattered across the region.

Major Brackett was placed in command of the district, with his headquarters in Sioux City, while General Sully was engaged in peace talks with Indian leaders. Later Sully traveled to St. Louis. Earlier in the spring, before Sully's expedition marched out of Fort Sully, Brackett initiated a letter to Senator Ramsey urging him to use his influence to have the battalion discharged from service upon their return from the campaign. But now it seemed the request had fallen on deaf ears.

Company C, at Fort Randall, was now distraught over the possibility of Captain Neely returning to command and the news that General Sully intended to keep the battalion in the district for the winter. In October the company drafted another petition to make a plea for their release—this time to General William T. Sherman in the East.

The lengthy letter covered six points of argument supporting their appeal:

> 1st    We are a veteran organization. . . . When we enlisted at Polaski, Tennessee, January 1, 1864, Government Recruiting Officers in addressing the troops upon this subject said, "Veterans would be the first troops discharged after the close of the war." . . .
>
> 2nd    For the two and one-half years we were connected with the 5th Iowa Cavalry, we understand that regiment has been out of the service several weeks. It was against the wishes of the enlisted men that we were detached from that regiment.
>
> 3rd    Since the war was ended, we have been constantly in the field. . . .
>
> 4th    About one-half of us are heads of families. We know that during the long cold winters, in Minnesota, that have passed since we enlisted, our families have suffered on account of our absence. Shall they be compelled to suffer and endure still more? . . .
>
> 5th    We believe we may be mustered out of service without injury to our country, cause or endangering the frontier.
>
> 6th    Have we not served our country as faithfully and honorably as our comrades of the 5th Iowa?[8]

A copy of the petition was sent to General Sully for his approval, which of course he declined to give. Like all their other attempts, the appeal produced no results.

With the approach of winter, the separated detachments of Brackett's Battalion carried out their patrol duties from their posts on the frigid, windswept prairie. The officers were allowed the privilege of having their families join them on the open plains. In one case, this courtesy nearly cost the lives of the officer's family and two of his men.

Captain Ara Barton arranged for his family to travel to St. Peter, Minnesota, which would not be too far from Dakota Territory. After Company D was posted at the fort at Sioux Falls, Barton made preparations for his family to come to the fort to be with him for the winter. At the end of November, Barton detailed two of his men, Corporal George Beebe and Private John McCole, to retrieve his wife and four children.

Both Beebe and McCole had served with Barton in Company F of the First Minnesota Mounted Rangers in 1863. The military had become Beebe's new family. His mother died sometime before the war, and his father died during the first year of the war. In 1862, at the age of fifteen, George traveled to Iowa to enlist. His officers discovered his true age after he had served three months and promptly sent him home to Minnesota. Two of George's brothers, both under the age of fifteen, had also enlisted, but successfully. Later in 1862 George's older brother and his brother's son were killed by Indians in Minnesota. His brother's wife and two other children survived.

Still only fifteen, George tried again to enlist, this time with the first Minnesota Mounted. He succeeded and served with the regiment during the 1863 campaign into Dakota Territory, which resulted in the battles of Big Mound, Dead Buffalo Lake, and Stony Lake. When the regiment mustered out in the fall of 1863, George followed Ara Barton to form a new company, which became Company D of Brackett's Battalion.

Sometimes George found himself at the wrong place at the wrong time. In the spring of 1863 when the First Mounted was posted at Fort Snelling, he was seriously injured when he was trampled by a drunken soldier and his horse. At the battle of Killdeer Mountain, he lost his hearing in both ears while fighting in front of firing artillery. From then on he could not hear the commands of his officers. When on the march, he would watch the movements of the men in front of him to understand what he needed to do.

In the late fall of 1865, Captain Barton impressed upon Corporal Beebe, now eighteen, and Private McCole, twenty-six, his desire to have his family join him as soon as possible. The two men left Sioux Falls on the first of December. They arrived at St. Peter on the fifth, having covered the 150 miles much faster than a company of cavalry could have done. They spent the next five days making preparations to convey the captain's wife and children to Sioux Falls. On the eleventh, the party began their journey with the family and luggage in a wagon driven by one of the men.

In the morning of the next day, the wagon team stopped at a small stream that was lightly frozen over. The team refused to move because it could see the water flowing under the ice, which presented a strange sight. Corporal Beebe climbed off the wagon and used his feet to break up the ice so the animals could see that the stream was not deep or threatening. The team then willingly crossed the stream, and the party continued on. The weather was mild, and so Beebe ignored his wet feet. But late in the morning a snowstorm set in followed by a quick drop in temperature and increase in wind speed.

The party picked up their pace to try to cover as much ground as possible. But the storm grew more severe. By late afternoon the snow was too deep to travel through, the wagon team was exhausted, and the party had come to a halt—stranded. They were in the middle of the open prairie in a vast sea of deep snow covering the land as far as the eye could see in any direction. To the best of their knowledge, there was no farmstead or settlement nearby. That night and the entire next day, the two cavalrymen and the captain's family huddled in the wagon under blankets and one buffalo robe. But the temperature became unbearable. Mrs. Barton and three of the children could not stay warm, and Corporal Beebe's feet and hands had frozen.

McCole began to make calculations. He realized that the town of Jackson was only about fourteen miles to the south. After a second night in the wagon, McCole set out alone on the morning of the fourteenth for Jackson. The rest of the party waited, wondering if they would see McCole or anyone again. In the afternoon of the same day, to their surprise, McCole and a man with a horse-drawn sleigh returned. The party was taken to Jackson where everyone received medical attention. The caption's wife and three of the children were treated for exposure; the fourth child was in good condition. The doctor treated Beebe's hands and feet and determined that his hands would recover but his feet were in bad condition. The doctor decided that Beebe's right foot could be saved, but the toes on the left were too far gone, and so they were amputated.

After spending time in Jackson recovering from the ordeal, McCole and the family finally completed their trip to the fort at Sioux Falls. Beebe was taken to nearby Spirit Lake, Iowa, to be treated at a hospital. He remained there for the entire winter.

That winter the men of the scattered companies of Brackett's Battalion lived like Eskimos on the frozen Arctic. Many of them traded their army coats to Indians for buffalo robes that they made into coats. Meanwhile Major Brackett was brevetted lieutenant colonel and in March 1866 was brevetted colonel. Finally in April the long-awaited news arrived. The battalion was to report to Fort Snelling to be mustered out. At Sioux Falls, Company D began making preparations for their departure. At the end of the month, Corporal Beebe arrived to rejoin his comrades. He was hobbling on crutches, his right foot still painful and his hands not fully recovered. A few days later, the company marched out of the fort. Upon their departure, two local newspapers published glowing editorials praising the long and faithful service of Brackett's Battalion. One editor wrote, "And, indeed, their services have been of no ordinary character. They have marched and fought over nearly the whole length of the continent. . . . Both men and officers will be long and favorably remembered by our citizens."[9]

But praises from the press did little to boost the spirits of the men. They had been kept from their families and homes longer than what they deserved. Marching into the compound of Fort Snelling in May, the men were in no mood for high praises. They were tired, weathered, and somewhat bitter. The horses, horse equipment, arms, and various other accouterments were turned in to the quartermaster.

Beginning on May 16, the men were mustered out of service in small groups, generally by companies. Anton Simonette, the first Minnesotan to be mustered in for cavalry service when the call to arms was sounded, was mustered out with most of the men in his company. On June 1, 1866, the remainder of Brackett's Battalion, men from Company B, were mustered out, disappearing into society.

Taking into consideration the time from when Anton Simonette was mustered into service in September 1861 to June 1, 1866, when the last men of the second company were mustered out, Brackett's Battalion, as a unit, served longer than any other Minnesota volunteers—four years and nine months. Though their extended service after the end of the Civil War was performed less than willingly, their discipline in carrying out their duty placed them in special company with those Union troops who served the longest. Only eight volunteer regiments in the entire Union army served longer than Brackett's Battalion.

In the throes of a nation in civil war, the first Minnesota cavalrymen who came to be known as Brackett's Battalion served across the face of the conflict against two vastly different enemies. In defense of their homes, the veteran cavalrymen marched across the broad, unforgiving expanse of the northwestern prairie against Native Americans in the beginnings of a war that would last for another two decades. As untried volunteers, they faced their own kind in the South to play a part in the abolition of slavery and the preservation of the United States.

They were "citizen soldiers" who answered the call of their country and state, suffered brutal hardships, and withstood the test of time, serving longer than most. Several years later Sergeant Isaac Botsford, a proud veteran, wrote, "When the men of Brackett's Battalion laid down the saber they took up the duties of the citizen, have built up and established homes for themselves, and are an honor to the communities in which they reside. Good soldiers! Good citizens! May we all meet in the great camp above."[10]

# Citizen Soldiers as Citizens

ON ARRIVING HOME, the men of Brackett's Battalion resumed their lives and careers. Many returned to their farms to rebuild what their families struggled to keep during the long absence and renew their partnership with nature. Those who left the family farm as enthusiastic young men, eagerly pursuing the life of a heroic cavalryman, returned home older, more mature, hardened by war, seeking to put the past behind them, but now better able to cope with hard rural life. The shopkeepers, clerks, factory workers, and those with professional careers in the cities and towns who once had little experience on a horse now returned to their communities as experienced horsemen, but with little prospect of ever utilizing that means of transportation again.

Eugene Marshall, who recorded much of the history of Brackett's Battalion in his war diaries, came home to Caledonia, Minnesota, where he married his longtime sweetheart, Lizzie, in November 1866. There they took up farming and raised a family of four children. In 1869, Eugene moved his family to Iowa with the hope of building a more successful farming venture. In Hancock County, Marshall pursued other opportunities as well. He was county superintendent of schools for two years, county surveyor for four years, and a deputy in the county treasurer's office.

But Eugene and Lizzie missed their old home. In 1880 they returned to Caledonia where Eugene managed a bank for seventeen more years. He continued to pursue his love of reading and writing. He resumed his diary writing and frequently corresponded with many of his old comrades of Brackett's Battalion. In 1895, his beloved Lizzie passed away at the age of fifty-two. Two years later Eugene retired at the age of sixty-five.

But retirement for the old former cavalryman soon changed to boredom. His thoughts often turned to Tennessee, where he had traveled and fought as a younger man. In 1899 Marshall moved to Manchester, Tennessee, where he bought a small farm in the area of the long-ago Tullahoma Campaign and a few miles southeast of Wartrace where he once led his company at the head of the Fifth Iowa Cavalry in a charge against a Confederate brigade. There Marshall found contentment. In 1919, Sergeant Major Eugene Marshall died in the land that claimed the lives of many Americans during the Civil War. He was sent back to Caledonia, the settlement he helped to establish, where he was buried beside his wife.

Most of the men of Brackett's Battalion resumed quiet, unassuming lives. For a few, the fame of being a Union cavalryman and their ambition to pursue public careers led them to loftier positions. Three men served in the Minnesota legislature; others engaged in law enforcement.

Known as the "old major" to the men, Colonel Brackett returned to St. Paul to renew his career as deputy U.S. marshal. Alfred Bruce Brackett was born in New Market, New Hampshire, in 1826, the youngest of nine children. At the age of fifteen he moved to Boston, Massachusetts, where he engaged in the grocery business. In 1848, with a craving for adventure and riches, Brackett quickly responded to the discovery of gold in California. Rather than traveling overland on a long, grueling journey, he boarded a ship that would take him to the land of riches where he would join other gold seekers who came to be known as the "forty-niners."

But Brackett was not destined for wealth. After six years in California he made his way back to Boston. However, his quest for opportunity in a rapidly expanding nation could not keep him tied down in the East. In 1856, he arrived in the settlement of St. Paul in the rapidly growing Minnesota Territory. There he opened a store with the help of an ambitious entrepreneur by the name of C. W. Griggs. But after one year, Brackett landed an opportunity that fed his itch for activity.

In 1857 he was hired as deputy sheriff of Ramsey County, which launched him on a career that proved to be his calling and unknowingly provided a training ground for becoming a cavalry officer. Alfred served under three sheriffs before he was appointed as deputy U.S. marshal. In the years before the Civil War, he was involved in many of the state's famous criminal cases, developing a reputation as a "well-known manhunter."

Thomas M. Newson, a close friend of Brackett, once wrote,

"Maj. Brackett's success in capturing a prisoner is brought about by his firmness and his kindness . . . with great energy of character, quiet in his movements and very decided and emphatic in his acts. With all this he is mild and lenient. He is a man of wonderful industry, has been and is now always on the go, and as a soldier he was prompt, brave and full of activity. He is as well known throughout the Northwest as any man in it, for there is scarcely a village or hamlet he has not visited in pursuit of some criminal. He is a man of large heart and sympathies, and socially very much liked.[1]

Two months after his discharge from the army, Brackett was married for the first time. He and his wife, Mary Elizabeth, had two daughters and one son. Tragically, Alfred lost his wife in 1871 after she had given birth to their son. In 1875, he married Mary's sister, Martha ("Mattie"), with whom he had a third daughter, Elizabeth.

Alfred served as deputy U.S. marshal until his death on September 22, 1892, at the age of sixty-six. Mattie died in 1920. Today, Mary and Martha rest one on each side of Colonel Brackett at Roselawn Cemetery in Roseville, Minnesota.

Brackett's "large heart and sympathies" showed through not only in his work as a law man but during his military service as well. While in the South, Major Brackett had enlisted the services of an elderly black woman, a former slave by the name of Millie Bronson, who became his cook. "Aunt Millie," as she was known, "was with him in all his skirmishes and battles," Newson wrote. "On their way through the South, Aunt Millie, wearing a Union soldier's coat, reached her old home and met some of her old friends who tried to persuade her to remain with them, but she exclaimed—'No, I'se gwine with Massa Lincoln's army of de Lord.' "[2]

Aunt Millie, believed to be more than ninety years old at the time, came to Minnesota with Brackett when the three companies of Minnesota cavalry returned home on veterans' furlough in February 1864. Even though Millie was a woman of great energy, Brackett, considering her age and the prospects of a long and arduous march in Dakota Territory, left Millie with his distant cousin George A. Brackett.

George was a wealthy Minneapolis entrepreneur and philanthropist. Many considered him to be one of the shakers and builders of Minneapolis, where he was elected mayor in 1872. During the Civil

War, George provided supplies and transportation for some of the Minnesota volunteer army units.

George engaged Millie as a nanny for his eleven children, a challenging chore for even the youngest of nannies. She became a cherished part of the family and was deeply loved by everyone. She kept in contact with Alfred as much as possible. When George met Brackett's Battalion at St. Peter with supply wagons and mule teams in the spring of 1865, Aunt Millie came along to see her old friend the major before the battalion departed for a second season in Dakota Territory.

After a long and eventful life, Millie Bronson passed away in 1885. One of her last requests was to be buried next to "Massa George." Today she lies peacefully in the front of the George Brackett family burial plot near George and his wife at Lakewood Cemetery in Minneapolis, which was founded by George and became a place of rest for many prominent Minnesotans. Millie Bronson, a former slave, was the first person of color to be buried there. Her grave marker reads, "Millie Bronson, 1770–1885."

Van Garren, Major Brackett's valet, was another former slave who benefited from Brackett's employ. When Brackett and the troops of the Fifth Iowa Cavalry were camped near Huntsville, Alabama, Van searched the vicinity of his old home for his mother and other members of his family, but he never found them. It was his only regret upon leaving the South. When Brackett's Battalion was mustered out of service, Van chose to stay close to his friends of the Second Company, most of whom were from Blue Earth County.

Van managed to obtain a small tract of land in Sterling Township, Blue Earth County, where he built a cabin near the river. Over the years he gained deep respect from his neighbors. Much of the regard rose out of a serious diphtheria epidemic when Van nursed many of the pioneers through the ordeal. In later years, he ran a milk route for the Sterling Creamery. Van Garren died in April 1905 and was laid to rest in the Sterling Church Cemetery near twenty-some other veterans of the Civil War. Braving thick mud on the roads that spring, a large crowd of friends and acquaintances attended his funeral.

Other men of Brackett's Battalion also went on to engage in notable pursuits. John Bauer, who recovered from the severe wound he received during the skirmish at Lockridge Mill in Tennessee, spent the rest of his life extending the Christian kindness he had received from Mrs.

Lockridge who nursed him back to health. He firmly believed he was saved by the "Christian lady" so that he could continue the Lord's work. Bauer became a missionary circuit rider for the German Methodist Church on the Minnesota frontier. Most of his preaching took him along the Minnesota River valley and in the St. Paul–Woodbury area.

Bauer's captain, Henning von Minden who led the "German company," returned to his surveying career. Von Minden was born in 1826 in Flensburg in the duchies of Schleswig-Holstein on the Danish-German border. There was a military tradition in his family that included one ancestor who served in the Prussian cavalry. Henning grew up speaking both Danish and German, and later he learned Latin and English. He went on to study engineering at Christian Albrechts University in Kiel. But his education at the university was interrupted when the Schleswig-Holstein war for independence against the Danish monarchy began in 1848. He joined the German army and fought in numerous battles. In 1850 he was wounded at the battle of Idstedt where the Germans were defeated and which eventually brought an end to the revolution. Henning retuned to the university in Kiel to finish his studies, and in 1852 he graduated with a surveyor's degree.

In 1855 von Minden followed his fellow 48ers to America. Many of the more influential freedom fighters had fled Germany to the U.S. a few years earlier. Henning's longtime fiancée, Elise, arrived from Germany more than a year later, and the two were married in St. Paul in 1857. After his discharge from the Union army in 1866, von Minden was immediately engaged in surveying for a new road in Montana. He returned to Minnesota and worked on the development of several new communities in the state that blossomed in the years after the Civil War. Von Minden was also a key organizer in the  establishment of the Minnesota Department of the Grand Army of the Republic, a strong lobbying and assistance organization for the Union veterans. Corporal Charles Ashley Bennett of Brackett's Company D for a time was the commander of the Minnesota GAR while engaged as the editor of the *Granite Falls Journal.*

In 1871 von Minden served on the St. Paul Board of Education. That same year he made plans to visit his homeland in northern Germany, which had been independent from Danish rule since 1864. All plans and preparations for the trip were complete when suddenly and unexpectedly on December 25 he died in St. Paul. In 1873 Elise von

Minden left her husband's adopted homeland and with their three children returned to northern Germany.

The former captain of Brackett's Company C, Erwin Shelley, teamed up with von Minden to develop the GAR in Minnesota and became the department's first adjutant general. Shelley arrived in St. Paul in 1849 just after being discharged from the Third United States Dragoons with which he fought in the Mexican War. He is believed to be the first printer to locate permanently in Minnesota. He worked for several newspapers in the new settlement, such as the *Register,* the *Pioneer,* and the *Daily Democrat.* After the Civil War, Shelley returned to his printing career in St. Paul and was known to have been engaged in the work longer than any of his contemporaries. He is also credited with helping to map the city of Superior, Wisconsin.

Unfortunately it appears that Shelley never overcame his thirst for hard liquor. Late in life he resided at the Soldiers' Home near Minnehaha Park for about ten years. In the spring of 1904, the seventy-six-year-old veteran brought whiskey into the home, which was prohibited and which was promptly taken from him. Angered by this, Shelley left the home and found a bed at an old friend's lodging house in St. Paul. He stayed there for three nights while a search party roamed the city looking for him. On the evening of April 29, Shelley left the lodging house, and the next morning his body was found in the Mississippi River.

Sergeant Isaac Botsford of Brackett's Company B also returned to printing and publishing in the newspaper business. The newspaper he founded in the town of Blue Earth, the *Blue Earth City News,* went out of business in 1862 after one year of publication, a few changes in publishers, and a name change. Botsford settled in the town of Albert Lea, Minnesota, the home of his new bride, Maggie, whom he married in 1864 while on veterans' furlough. There he continued his love of publishing with the *Albert Lea Standard.* But his life's pursuit was cut short in 1878 when illness forced him to retire at the age of forty-two.

In 1889, Isaac was once again called upon to write. At the request of a board of commissioners, appointed by the Minnesota legislature, he drafted the first published narrative on the history of Brackett's Battalion for the book *Minnesota in the Civil and Indian Wars, 1861–1865,* published in 1890. Eugene Marshall was a major contributor to the narrative. Sergeant Botsford died two years later.

The trusted captain of Brackett's Company D, Ara Barton, continued to involve himself in public service. Once the lieutenant colonel of a regiment of state militia during Minnesota's first year of statehood, he served a term in the Minnesota House of Representatives in 1859. After his service with Brackett's Battalion, Barton served two more terms in the state legislature in 1871 and 1872. When he attached the title sheriff to his name, Barton became involved in one of the most famous incidents in the Northwest.

During Ara Barton's twelve-year tenure as sheriff of Rice County, Minnesota, on September 7, 1876, eight bandits of the James-Younger gang made an ill-fated attempt to rob the First National Bank in Northfield. Unable to gain entry to the safe, the outlaws engaged in a shootout in the street with well-armed citizens. After the smoke had cleared, one bank clerk was dead, another suffered wounds, a third citizen was shot fatally outside the bank, and two of the bandits lay dead in the street.

For two weeks large posses hunted the remainder of the gang across southern Minnesota. After another skirmish near Madelia, some eighty miles from Northfield, one more outlaw was killed, while Cole, James, and Bob Younger were captured. Jesse and Frank James managed to slip out of the state, never to be captured. The Younger brothers were brought to the Rice County jail at Faribault where they were placed in the custody of Sheriff Barton. All three of the brothers were badly wounded, Cole with seven bullet wounds alone.

In November the Younger brothers pleaded guilty to the charge of murder, thus avoiding a jury trial and the possibility of receiving the death sentence. They were then sentenced to life imprisonment and transferred to Stillwater State Prison. At Stillwater, the Youngers became model prisoners, never causing any trouble.

The prison's warden at the time was John A. Reed, former captain of Company B of Brackett's Battalion. Before taking charge of the prison, Reed had served three terms in the Minnesota legislature about the same time as Ara Barton after the war.

Cole Younger maintained a friendship with Barton. He had a flair for craftsmanship and produced many keepsakes for friends and acquaintances while incarcerated. Once he crafted a very fine leather cane for Sheriff Barton that included a brass tip on one end and a brass knob on the other. The cane remains in the family today.

Marshal Alfred Brackett also came to know the Younger brothers. He lived near the Stillwater prison for a short time and made frequent visits there in the course of his duties. During some visits, Brackett would bring along his youngest daughter, Elizabeth, who also struck up a friendly acquaintance with Cole Younger. For her, Cole produced a beautifully constructed jewelry box made of dark- and light-colored strips of wood with her initials inscribed on the top. This treasured gift from one of the most notorious criminals of the time also remains in Elizabeth's family.

Over the years, the veterans of Brackett's Battalion retained their comradeship. Through battalion reunions and GAR functions, the aging cavalrymen found it easier to share their war experiences with men who had been there with them. Many lived during an age of tremendous growth and vast changes in the world around them. As their numbers dwindled into the twentieth century, their stories of long marches and saber charges were left with surviving family members and historians. Some of the stories would never again be heard.

John Lenard McConnell of Company C of Brackett's Battalion was one of the few who lived to count the number of survivors. McConnell was born in Ayr County, Scotland, in 1846. In 1849 his family arrived in America, settling in Pennsylvania. After brief stays in Illinois and later Iowa, the McConnell family arrived in Minnesota Territory in 1854. They settled at Fort Ridgely on the lonely western frontier of the territory where John's father, Alexander, worked on government boats on the nearby Minnesota River and later was an engineer at the nearby sawmills. A few years later, the family staked a claim in Blakeley Township, Scott County, to begin a long struggle as farmers in a sparsely populated region of the state.

The family survived the terrors of the Dakota War of 1862. Shortly afterward, the forty-one-year-old Alexander volunteered for military service. John was too young for military duty at that time, but after turning seventeen he left his mother and sisters on the farm to join Brackett's Battalion at Fort Snelling in March 1864 while the battalion was there preparing for the Northwestern Indian Expedition. Just a few months later, the green trooper found himself in a battle with the Sioux at Killdeer Mountain in Dakota Territory. John's father was also on the battlefield as a sergeant with the Eighth Minnesota. In September, when the expedition returned to Fort Rice, both father and son received mail containing horrible news. They learned that John's mother had died more than two months earlier. In spite of their despair, John and Alexander remained loyal to their military commitment.

While Brackett's Battalion was in winter quarters at Fort Ridgely and John's father was engaged in hard campaigning against the Confederates in Tennessee, John realized the hardships his family was enduring on the farm: "I hope that the rain filled up your well. I hope that this will be an early spring for the good of soldier's families," John wrote in a letter to his sister Maggie in February 1865.

> I hope that we will all live to see us all happy. You must keep up your spirits until I get home and then I will atone for the past.
>
> I have been thinking how nice that I will fix up things when I get home. This is the way that I am going to fix up the house: lay the floors anew and make three rooms on the lower floor, a bedroom and a parlor and kitchen; then I will build a new addition on the back, then I will make three rooms upstairs and then have it plastered and painted and then I will build a board fence all along the road and plant trees around the house and have every thing nice.
>
> I think that the war will be over soon and then it will be a happy day to soldiers when they can come home and take care of the loved ones at home, so I hope that the time is near.
>
> I wrote a letter to father and sent him the stamps and one sheet of paper.[3]

John McConnell was discharged with Company C on May 24, 1866, nearly one year after his father's discharge. In 1872 he married Julia Sprague with whom he had four daughters and three sons. While working the family farm, John became involved in local government as well. Over the years he served as justice of the peace, township assessor, and township supervisor of Blakeley Township. John also became a lifetime member of the Masonic Lodge and the GAR.

Julia died in 1892 after giving birth to their third son. In 1895, John married his second wife, Nancy, who died in 1909. John retired from the family farm in Blakeley Township in 1913. That same year he married a Mrs. Sandberg, who died in 1916. Later he married his fourth wife, Helen, who died in 1939.

In 1939, after Helen's death, John traveled to North Dakota on a pilgrimage that he vowed long ago he would make. On the day of his ninety-third birthday, June 14, dressed in a suit and tie, McConnell walked the grounds of the battlefield at Killdeer Mountain where he and his father fought together seventy-five years earlier. John was the last known surviving veteran of the 1864 Northwestern Indian Expedition and the last man of Brackett's Battalion.

At the base of the high ridge once known as Brackett's Peak, McConnell drank the water of Falling Springs from which he and his comrades had quenched their thirst after the battle on that scorching hot July day. A local newspaperman was with McConnell at the site. The old veteran told of the agony the men and horses were in before they finally got relief from the sweet, cool waters of the spring: "The grasshoppers . . . had almost stripped the land of grass and foliage and the horses were gaunt from travel and lack of food. The heat was oppressive and drought had stricken the land making life miserable for both man and beast carrying war equipment."[4]

Surveying the grounds further, McConnell noticed an object in the soil that attracted his attention. It was too smooth to be a rock. After prying the heavy object from the dirt, he held in his hands an unexploded case-shot round once fired from one of the expedition's artillery pieces during the battle, a reminder of the carnage that had taken place there.

Finally, McConnell approached the site of two white marble slabs surrounded by a steel fence. He removed his hat and stood in silent reverence before the monuments of his fallen comrades George Northrup and Horatio Austin. The American Legion had provided the markers. The actual graves remain in an unknown location, kept secret by time. After paying his respects, McConnell departed for home.

Over the years John McConnell remained one of only a handful of surviving Union veterans of the Civil War living in Minnesota. The old soldiers would ride in open cars in Memorial Day parades. On their birthdays, local newspapers would publish glowing tributes to their lives and recount their experiences in the war. They became living monuments to an age long faded. In 1941, McConnell, age ninety-five, attended the GAR's National Encampment at Columbus, Ohio, the seventy-fifth anniversary of the GAR. It would be McConnell's last National Encampment. In 1943 at the age of ninety-seven, John L. McConnell left to join the rest of Brackett's Battalion in the "great camp above."

# ACKNOWLEDGMENTS

THIS PROJECT could not have been accomplished without the eager assistance of several individuals who contributed their time, research, advice, and support.

In the early stages of research, Roger A. Norland generously contributed numerous copies of newspaper articles, several of which were written by the men of Brackett's Battalion, from his ongoing research on Minnesota's Civil War history. By drawing on his extensive research, Roger became a key contributor to the development of the John Campbell story. Although a dark moment in the history of Brackett's Battalion, it is a compelling story that required serious attention in a history such as this.

Many other friends, acquaintances, longtime students of Civil War and cavalry history, and various historical institutions throughout the course of this project provided valuable sources, leads, and technical work, most notably the Minnesota Historical Society, Dave Arneson, Douglas W. Ellison, Dr. William C. Harralson, Stephen E. Osman, David L. Wood, and the members of Brackett's Battalion of Minnesota Volunteer Cavalry, Inc. Thank you one and all.

Special thanks to Christopher T. Brovold whose immediate and generous help made this project possible.

It is also my ancestors who served our country and who provided motivation for this project. The story of Brackett's Battalion is just one chapter in their legacy that began with the Revolutionary War and extended into the Civil War. The descendants of my Revolutionary War veteran ancestors and my German ancestors settled in the Upper Midwest. From there they left their families during the Civil War and went off to serve with the Sixth Wisconsin Infantry, the First Regiment of Minnesota Heavy Artillery, Brackett's Battalion of Minnesota Cavalry, and the Second Regiment of Minnesota Cavalry. It is their service and devotion to *their* country that has made the United States *our* nation.

# Notes

### The First Companies of Minnesota Cavalry in the Civil War

1. "Association of Survivors of Minnesota Battalion, Fifth Iowa Cavalry and Brackett's Battalion, Minnesota Cavalry," reunion newsletter, 1906, collection of DeWayne Torfin.
2. *St. Paul Pioneer and Democrat,* Nov. 5, 1861.
3. *Mankato Semi-Weekly Record,* Nov. 23, 1861.

### Cavalry Training at St. Louis and Joining a Regiment

1. *Mankato Semi-Weekly Record,* Jan. 22, 1862.
2. *St. Paul Pioneer and Democrat,* Jan. 25, 1862.
3. *Mankato Weekly Independent,* Feb. 5, 1862.
4. Clark G. Reynolds, "The Civil and Indian War Diaries of Eugene Marshall, Minnesota Volunteer" (master's thesis, Duke University, 1963), 85, copy in Minnesota Historical Society (hereafter MHS).

### Into the Fight at Last

1. Reynolds, "Eugene Marshall," 100.
2. Reynolds, "Eugene Marshall," 103.
3. Reynolds, "Eugene Marshall," 111.
4. Reynolds, "Eugene Marshall," 124.

### Shiloh and the Siege of Corinth

1. Isaac Botsford, "Narrative of Brackett's Battalion of Cavalry," in *Minnesota in the Civil and Indian Wars, 1861–1865* (St. Paul: Minnesota Board of Commissioners on Publication of History of Minnesota in the Civil and Indian Wars, 1890–93), 1:574.

### Disaster at Lockridge Mill

1. Reynolds, "Eugene Marshall," 157.
2. Botsford, "Brackett's Battalion," 1:576.

### A New Name for Curtis Horse

1. Reynolds, "Eugene Marshall," 168–70.

### Recapture of Clarksville

1. Reynolds, "Eugene Marshall," 208.
2. Reynolds, "Eugene Marshall," 211.
3. Reynolds, "Eugene Marshall," 217.
4. Lt. August Matthaus to Oscar Malmros, Minnesota Adjutant General, Report, Oct. 30, 1862, Adjutant General's index, Brackett's Battalion, State Archives, MHS.
5. Matthaus to Malmros, Report, Oct. 30, 1862.

### Attack on Dover · Von Minden Captured Again

1. Reynolds, "Eugene Marshall," 242.
2. Reynolds, "Eugene Marshall," 248.

### The Tullahoma Campaign

1. Reynolds, "Eugene Marshall," 260–61.
2. Reynolds, "Eugene Marshall," 261–62.
3. Reynolds, "Eugene Marshall," 262.

### Long Marches and Hard Charges

1. Reynolds, "Eugene Marshall," 281.
2. Reynolds, "Eugene Marshall," 278–79.
3. Reynolds, "Eugene Marshall," 280.
4. George W. Northrup to Alice Humphreys, Nov. 9, 1863, George W. Northrup Letters, MHS.
5. Reynolds, "Eugene Marshall," 277.
6. Reynolds, "Eugene Marshall," 284.
7. Reynolds, "Eugene Marshall," 282.
8. *Mankato Weekly Record,* Dec. 26, 1863.

### George W. Northrup

1. Northrup to Teresa E. Northrup, Dec. 12, 1853, Northrup Letters.
2. Northrup to Teresa Northrup, Mar. 11, 1854, Northrup Letters.
3. Gertrude W. Ackermann, "George Northrup, Frontier Scout," *Minnesota History* 19 (Dec. 1938): 377–92; *Daily Minnesotian,* July 18, 1860.
4. Edward Eggleston, with William P. Randel, "The Kit Carson of the Northwest," *Minnesota History* 33 (Autumn 1953): 269–81.

### Sully's Troops March

1. *Mankato Weekly Record,* May 21, 1864.
2. *St. Paul Weekly Press,* May 12, 1864.
3. Reynolds, "Eugene Marshall," 296.

### Battle of Killdeer Mountain

1. Reynolds, "Eugene Marshall," 312.
2. Reynolds, "Eugene Marshall," 312.
3. Reynolds, "Eugene Marshall," 312.
4. Don Diessner, *Sitting Bull's Story: There Are No Indians Left But Me!* (El Segundo, Calif.: Upton and Sons, 1993), 44.
5. Diessner, *Sitting Bull's Story,* 44.
6. Diessner, *Sitting Bull's Story,* 45.
7. Diessner, *Sitting Bull's Story,* 44.
8. *Mankato Review,* Dec. 15, 1891.
9. Reynolds, "Eugene Marshall," 314.
10. Eugene Marshall to *St. Paul Weekly Press,* Aug. 1, 1864, copy in Brackett Papers.
11. Diessner, *Sitting Bull's Story,* 44.
12. Col. Robert N. McLaren, Report, July 29, 1864, *Minnesota in the Civil and Indian Wars,* 2:543.

### Battle through the Badlands

1. Brig. Gen. Alfred Sully, Report, Aug. 18[?], 1864, *Minnesota in the Civil and Indian Wars,* 2:530.
2. Marshall to *St. Paul Weekly Press,* Aug. 13, 1864, copy in Brackett Papers.
3. Sully, Report, Aug. 18[?], 1864, *Minnesota in the Civil and Indian Wars,* 2:530.
4. Reynolds, "Eugene Marshall," 325.
5. Diessner, *Sitting Bull's Story,* 45.
6. Marshall to *St. Paul Weekly Press,* Aug. 13, 1864, copy in Brackett Papers.
7. Marshall to *St. Paul Weekly Press,* Aug. 13, 1864, copy in Brackett Papers.

8. Maj. A. B. Brackett to Capt. John H. Pell, Aug. 13, 1864, *Minnesota in the Civil and Indian Wars,* 2:536.
9. Sully, Report, Aug. 13, 1864, *Minnesota in the Civil and Indian Wars,* 2:532.
10. Marshall to *St. Paul Weekly Press,* Aug. 13, 1864, copy in Brackett Papers.
11. Marshall to *St. Paul Weekly Press,* Aug. 13, 1864, copy in Brackett Papers.
12. Reynolds, "Eugene Marshall," 337.
13. Reynolds, "Eugene Marshall," 337.
14. Reynolds, "Eugene Marshall," 338.
15. Reynolds, "Eugene Marshall," 340.

### Captain Fisk's Perilous Wagon Train

1. Willoughby Wells, "Brackett's Battalion of Minnesota Cavalry, Company B," 1945, vol. 35, Genealogical Records, Duluth, Daughters of the American Revolution, Minnesota, Genealogical Collection, MHS.
2. Wells, "Brackett's Battalion."
3. Wells, "Brackett's Battalion."
4. Helen McCann White, *Ho! for the Gold Fields: Northern Overland Wagon Trains of the 1860s* (St. Paul: Minnesota Historical Society, 1966), 143.
5. Wells, "Brackett's Battalion."
6. Wells, "Brackett's Battalion."
7. Wells, "Brackett's Battalion."
8. Wells, "Brackett's Battalion."
9. Wells, "Brackett's Battalion."

### Extended Service: The Expedition of 1865

1. Reynolds, "Eugene Marshall," 360.
2. Major Alfred B. Brackett to Sergeant Major Eugene Marshall, Mar. 23, 1865, collection of Eugene A. Buelow and Jerold H. Buelow.
3. Reynolds, "Eugene Marshall," 366.
4. Reynolds, "Eugene Marshall," 377.
5. Charles Ashley Bennett, diary, 1865, MHS.
6. Eugene Marshall, diary, Special Collections Library, Duke University.
7. Reynolds, "Eugene Marshall," 393.
8. Petition in Brackett Papers.
9. Botsford, "Brackett's Battalion," 1:584.
10. Botsford, "Brackett's Battalion," 1:584.

### Citizen Soldiers as Citizens

1. Thomas M. Newson, *Pen Pictures of St. Paul, Minnesota, and Biographical Sketches of Old Settlers* (St. Paul, 1886), 596.
2. Newson, *Pen Pictures,* 596.
3. John McConnell Papers, collection of Dorothy Ward.
4. *Killdeer Herald,* June 15, 1939.

# Bibliography

Ackermann, Gertrude W. "George Northrup, Frontier Scout." *Minnesota History* 19 (Dec. 1938): 377–92.

Anderson, Gary Clayton, and Alan R. Woolworth, eds. *Through Dakota Eyes: Narrative Accounts of the Minnesota Indian War of 1862.* St. Paul: Minnesota Historical Society Press, 1988. Personal accounts of the 1862 Dakota War by the siblings of John L. Campbell.

*Blue Earth City News,* Nov. 1861–July 1862.

Brackett, Herbert I. *Brackett Genealogy.* Washington, D.C.: H. I. Brackett, 1907.

"Brackett's Battalion: Two Routes to be Opened to Montana and Idaho." *St. Paul Pioneer,* May 16, 1865.

"The Campbell Family–Sketch of John Campbell–The Action of Judge Lynch Justified." *St. Paul Pioneer,* May 7, 1865.

Carley, Kenneth. *The Dakota War of 1862: Minnesota's Other Civil War.* St. Paul: Minnesota Historical Society Press, 1961, 1976. Originally published as *The Sioux Uprising of 1862.*

Diessner, Don. *Sitting Bull's Story: There Are No Indians Left But Me!* El Segundo, Calif.: Upton and Sons, 1993. The quotations from Sitting Bull used in this history are made possible by permission of the publisher.

Dyer, Frederick H. *A Compendium of the War of the Rebellion.* Des Moines: Dyer Pub. Co., 1908.

Edwards, William B. *Civil War Guns.* Secaucus, N.J.: Book Sales, 1982. Contains account of the formation of the Frémont Hussars.

Eggleston, Edward, with William P. Randel. "The Kit Carson of the Northwest." *Minnesota History* 33 (Autumn 1953): 269–81.

English, Abner M. "Dakota's First Soldiers: History of the First Dakota Cavalry, 1862–1865." *South Dakota Historical Collections.* Vol. 11. Pierre: South Dakota State Historical Society, 1918.

Ezell, John S. "Excerpts from the Civil War Diary of Lieutenant Charles Alley, Company C, Fifth Iowa Cavalry." *Iowa Journal of History* 49 (1951).

Folwell, William Watts. *A History of Minnesota.* Vol. 2. St. Paul: Minnesota Historical Society, 1924, 1961.

*Frontier Scout.* July 20, Aug. 17, 31, 1865, copies in Brackett Papers.

Graber, John W. "One Man's Civil War." *Minnesota History* 52 (Winter 1990): 144–45. The story of John Bauer, wounded at Lockridge Mill.

Hart, Herbert M. *Old Forts of the Northwest.* Seattle: Superior Pub. Co., 1963.

——. *Pioneer Forts of the West.* Seattle: Superior Pub. Co., 1967.

Hassrick, Royal B. *The Sioux: Life and Customs of a Warrior Society.* Norman: University of Oklahoma Press, 1964.

Heck, Frank H. "The Grand Army of the Republic in Minnesota, 1866–80." *Minnesota History* 16 (Dec. 1935): 427–44. Provides information about the roles of veterans of Brackett's Battalion in the Minnesota GAR.

Herr, John K., and Edward S. Wallace. *The Story of the U.S. Cavalry, 1775–1942.* New York: Bonanza Books, 1953, 1984.

Hughes, Thomas. *History of Blue Earth County.* Chicago: Middle West Pub. Co., 1909.

——. *Indian Chiefs of Southern Minnesota.* Mankato: Free Press, 1927; Minneapolis: Ross and Haines, 1969. Contains an account of the brothers of John L. Campbell during the 1862 Dakota War.

Innis, Ben. *A Chronological Record of Events at the Missouri-Yellowstone Confluence Area from 1805 to 1896, and A Record of Interments at the Fort Buford, Dakota Territory, Post Cemetery, 1866 to 1895.* Williston, N.D.: Fort Buford 6th Infantry Regiment Assn., 1971.

Iowa Adjutant General. *Report of the Adjutant General and Acting Quartermaster General of the State of Iowa.* Vol. 2. Des Moines, 1865. History of the Fifth Iowa Regiment of Cavalry.

Josephy, Alvin M., Jr. *The Civil War in the American West.* New York: Alfred A. Knopf, 1991.

Kiester, Jacob A. *The History of Faribault County, Minnesota.* Minneapolis: Harrison and Smith, 1896. Contains a biography of Isaac Botsford.

Kingsbury, David L. "Sully's Expedition Against the Sioux in 1864." In *Collections of the Minnesota Historical Society.* Vol. 8, p. 449–62. St. Paul: Minnesota Historical Society, 1898.

Marshall, Eugene. "Brackett's Battalion. The Great Northwestern Indian Expedition of 1864." *St. Paul Pioneer Press,* Jan. 25, 1897.

Mattison, Ray H. "Fort Union: Its Role in the Upper Missouri Fur Trade." *North Dakota History* 29 (Jan.–Apr. 1962).

Minnesota Adjutant General. *Annual Report of the Adjutant General of the State of Minnesota.* St. Paul, 1866. Rosters of all Minnesota volunteer units formed during the Civil War.

Minnesota Board of Commissioners on Publication of History of Minnesota in the Civil and Indian Wars. *Minnesota in the Civil and Indian Wars, 1861–1865.* 2 vols. St. Paul, 1890. Vol. 1 contains narrative histories of Brackett's Battalion, Eighth Minnesota Infantry, Hatch's Battalion of Cavalry, Second Minnesota Cavalry, and Third Minnesota Battery, as well as all other Minnesota volunteer units formed during the Civil War. Vol. 2 consists of the "Official Reports and Correspondence."

Moe, Richard. *The Last Full Measure: The Life and Death of the First Minnesota Volunteers.* New York: Henry Holt and Co., 1993; St. Paul: Minnesota Historical Society Press, 2001.

Newson, Thomas M. *Pen Pictures of St. Paul, Minnesota, and Biographical Sketches of Old Settlers.* St. Paul, 1886. Provides biographies of Alfred B. Brackett, Erwin Y. Shelley, and Millie Bronson.

150 Years of German Revolution. Germany: Hesperian Press, 1999.

Potter, Theodore E. "Captain Potter's Recollections of Minnesota Experiences." *Minnesota History Bulletin* 1 (Nov. 1916): 419–521. Contains an account of the Jewett family murders (503–5).

Quiner, E. B. *The Military History of Wisconsin*. Chicago: Clarke and Co., 1866.

Reuter, Kelly Dethloff. *Amboy, Minnesota: A Heritage Rooted in Rural America*. Amboy, 1979. Includes some information on Van Garren.

Rodenbough, Theo. F., ed. *The Photographic History of the Civil War*. Vol. 2, *The Decisive Battles, The Cavalry*. Secaucus, N.J.: Blue and Grey Press, 1987.

Rose, Arthur P. *An Illustrated History of Jackson County, Minnesota*. Jackson: Northern History Pub. Co., 1910.

*Roster and Record of Iowa Soldiers in the War of the Rebellion*. 6 vols. Des Moines, 1910. Vol. 4 contains another variation of the history of the Fifth Iowa Regiment of Cavalry.

*St. Paul Weekly Press,* May 12–June 9, 1864. Contains articles by George Northrup.

Shea, William L., and Earl J. Hess. *Pea Ridge: Civil War Campaign in the West*. Chapel Hill: University of North Carolina Press, 1992. Contains biography of Gen. Samuel R. Curtis and accounts of military conflicts and activities in Missouri in 1861.

Starr, Stephen Z. *The Union Cavalry in the Civil War*. Vol. 3, *The War in the West, 1861–1865*. Baton Rouge: Louisiana State University Press, 1985. Provides accounts of the Tullahoma Campaign of 1863, Gen. Joseph Wheeler's raid across central Tennessee in 1863, and status of the Fifth Iowa Cavalry.

Trenerry, Walter N. *Murder in Minnesota: A Collection of True Cases*. St. Paul: Minnesota Historical Society Press, 1962, 1985. Accounts of early Minnesota criminal cases involving Deputy Sheriff, later Deputy Marshal, Alfred B. Brackett and James-Younger gang raid at Northfield, Minn.

United States. War Department. *The War of the Rebellion: A Compilation of the Official Records of the Union and Confederate Armies*. Washington, D.C.: GPO, 1880–1901.

Ward, Geoffrey C., with Ric Burns and Ken Burns. *The Civil War: An Illustrated History*. New York: Alfred A. Knopf, 1990.

White, Helen McCann. *Ho! For the Gold Fields–Northern Overland Wagon Trains of the 1860s*. St. Paul: Minnesota Historical Society, 1966. Contains detailed accounts of the Thomas Holmes and James L. Fisk wagon train expeditions.

Williams, J. Fletcher. *A History of the City of Saint Paul to 1875*. 1876; St. Paul: Minnesota Historical Society Press, 1983. Additional information on John L. Campbell.

Williams, Major George F. *The Memorial War Book*. New York: Dreyfus Pub. Co., 1894.

Wills, Brian Steel. *A Battle from the Start: The Life of Nathan Bedford Forrest*. New York: HarperCollins, 1992.

#### Unpublished Works and Additional Sources

Adjutant General's index, "Brackett's Battalion," official communications, correspondence, reports, muster documents, including a compilation of manuscripts by Eugene Marshall, State Archives, Minnesota Historical Society (hereafter MHS), St. Paul.

"Association of Survivors of Minnesota Battalion, Fifth Iowa Cavalry and Brackett's Battalion, Minnesota Cavalry." Reunion newsletters of 1906, 1908, and 1910. DeWayne Torfin collection.

Barton, Ara. Papers. Warde H. Barton collection. Certificate of commission of Ara Barton as lieutenant colonel of the Thirteenth Minnesota Militia, newspaper accounts, and other papers pertaining to Sheriff Ara Barton's association with Cole, James, and Bob Younger.

Beebe, George W. Papers. Collection of Tim Meyer.

Bennett, Charles Ashley. Diary, 1865, MHS. Company D, Brackett's Battalion.

Brackett, Alfred B. Papers. MHS. Chronological list of events of the Minnesota companies of the Fifth Iowa Cavalry and Brackett's Battalion.

——. Family Bible, 1868. Collection of Barbara Fairchild Gramm.

——. Letter to Sergeant Major Eugene Marshall, March 23, 1865. Collection of Eugene A. Buelow and Jerold H. Buelow.

Brackett, Russell D. "The Story of George Augustus Brackett (1836–1921) and His Descendants." MHS.

Campbell, S. S. Diary transcript, 1864–1865. North Dakota State Historical Society, Bismarck. Company D, Brackett's Battalion.

Ellison, Douglas W. "Circle the Wagons: The Siege at Fort Dilts." Manuscript, courtesy Douglas W. Ellison. Account of the 1864 James L. Fisk wagon train expedition.

Garen, Florence. Papers. Collection of Douglas J. Stolzman.

Hoy, George T., and Hugh A. Hoy. Biographies. Collection of Robert Wickman.

Larned, William. Family Papers, 1849–1967. MHS. Larned's diary provides an account of the 1864 James L. Fisk wagon train with which he traveled as one of the settlers.

Lowe, William W. Military resume. Bureau of Library and Archives, State Historical Society of Iowa, Des Moines.

Marshall, Eugene. Diaries of 1864–65. Special Collections Library, Duke University, Durham.

——. "Narrative of the Civil War, 1861–62," 1909. MHS. Narrative of the Minnesota companies of the Fifth Iowa Cavalry.

McConnell, John L. Papers. Dorothy Bullert collection.

——. Papers. Dorothy Ward collection.

National Archives and Records Administration. Civil Reference Branch. Service record of Deputy U.S. Marshal Alfred B. Brackett.

——. General Reference Branch (NNRG). Military service records of several members of Brackett's Battalion.

Neely, Mortimer. "Narrative of Company C, Brackett's Battalion." MHS. Notes on dated events.

Norland, Roger A. "Common Men, Uncommon Times, Blue Earth County in the Civil and Indian Wars, 1861–1865," 1990. Courtesy Roger A. Norland. Story of Van Garren.

Northrup, George W. Letters, 1852–64. MHS. Letters to relatives and wartime pen pal Alice Humphreys.

Reynolds, Clark G. "The Civil and Indian War Diaries of Eugene Marshall, Minnesota Volunteer." Master's thesis, Duke University, 1963.

Shelley, Erwin Y. Papers. Collection of Roger A. Norland.

"Sixth Confederate States Cavalry." Harold B. Simpson Confederate Research Center, Hillsboro, Tex.

von Minden, Henning. Papers. Collection of Jutta Stahl-Strelitz, Hamburg, Germany.

Wells, Willoughby. "Brackett's Battalion of Minnesota Cavalry, Company B," 1945, vol. 35. Genealogical Records, Duluth, Daughters of the American Revolution, Minnesota, Genealogical Collection, MHS. Personal account of the 1864 James L. Fisk wagon train.

# Index

PICTURE CREDITS

New York State Library, Albany—page 78 (bottom left)
Minnesota Historical Society, St. Paul—page 78 (top, bottom right), 79 (top, bottom right and left), 82, 83 (middle), 85 (both)
Missouri Historical Society, St. Louis—page 81 (bottom; A. McLean, lithograph)
Duke University, Special Collections Library—page 80
Washington County Historical Society, Stillwater, Minn.—page 83 (top)
Warde H. Barton Collection—page 83 (bottom)
Dorothy Ward Collection—page 86

The maps are by David L. Wood.

*Brackett's Battalion* was designed and set in type at the Minnesota Historical Society Press by Will Powers. The text typeface is Monticello. This book was printed by Maple Press, York, Pennsylvania.

Printed in the USA
CPSIA information can be obtained
at www.ICGtesting.com
JSHW082203140824
68134JS00014B/410